The American Victorian Woman

Recent Titles in Contributions in Women's Studies

THE AMERICAN VICTORIAN WOMAN

THE MYTH AND THE REALITY

Mabel Collins Donnelly

Foreword by
Carol C. Nadelson

CONTRIBUTIONS IN WOMEN'S STUDIES, NUMBER 71

Greenwood Press
NEW YORK · WESTPORT, CONNECTICUT · LONDON

Library of Congress Cataloging-in-Publication Data

Donnelly, Mabel Collins.
 The American Victorian woman.

 (Contributions in women's studies, ISSN 0147-104X ;
no. 71)
 Bibliography: p.
 Includes index.
 1. Women—United States—Social conditions.
2. Women—United States—Economic conditions.   I. Title.
II. Series.
HQ1426.D79   1986   305.4'2'0973   86-358
ISBN: 0-313-25327-7 (lib. bdg. : alk. paper)
ISBN: 0-313-25696-9 (pkb.)

Library of Congress Catalog Card Number: 86-358
ISBN: 0-313-25327-7
ISBN: 0-313-25696-9 (paperback)
ISSN: 0147-104X

First published in 1986

Greenwood Press, Inc.
88 Post Road West, Westport, Connecticut 06881

Printed in the United States of America

The paper used in this book complies with the
Permanent Paper Standard issued by the National
Information Standards Organization (Z39.48-1984).

10 9 8 7 6 5 4 3 2 1

For
Mavis Joan Donnelly
and
James Manning Donnelly

I come forth to speak 'bout Woman's Rights. . . . I know that it feels a kind o' hissin' and ticklin' like to see a colored woman get up and tell you about things, and Woman's Rights. We have all been thrown down so low that nobody thought we'd ever get up again.

Sojourner Truth, speech, 1853

Conceive of never being without the sense that if you let yourself go for a moment your mechanism will fall into pie and that at some given moment you must abandon it all, let the dykes break and the flood sweep in, acknowledging yourself abjectly impotent before the immutable laws.

Alice James, *The Diary of Alice James,* October 26, 1890

Hannah Arendt has observed that government is upheld by power supported either through consent or imposed through violence. Conditioning to an ideology amounts to the former. Sexual politics obtains consent through the "socialization" of both sexes to basic patriarchal politics with regard to temperament, role and status.

Kate Millett, *Sexual Politics,* 1970

My aim is to integrate psychoanalysis with history. . . . Perhaps the most distinctive quality of this kind of history lies in its receptivity to the conspicuous share of the social world in the making of minds, even in their unconscious workings.

Peter Gay, *The Bourgeois Experience,* 1984

CONTENTS

FOREWORD

Myths and stereotypes are pervasive. The fact that they so often cross cultures attests to their tenacity and universality as well as to the wishes and vulnerabilities they hide. Although they change in form and content, they persist and affect our attitudes, expectations, and behaviors. While we no longer perceive dysmennorhea as the inevitable burden of women because they are the "weaker" sex, or as a punishment for sexual wishes or activity, we have not yet given up our enthusiasm for embracing myth as reality. We continue to assume that most women have physical and emotional symptoms related specifically to their menses, and that menopausal women are more at risk for depression, despite the lack of evidence to support either belief.

In failing to appreciate the exquisite interaction between mind and body, we continue to stigmatize those with some kinds of symptoms at the same time as we overread, overgeneralize and overtreat other symptoms, especially those affecting women. We are impelled, in part, by our awe and ambivalence about women's reproductive power. Women's psychology and biology have traditionally been linked in ways that fail to realistically take account of their diversity and difference. While men do not experience the ticking of the biological clock, that does not imply that women *are* their biology or, as Freud put it, that anatomy is destiny. Women's choices today embrace a broader scope of life experience and expectation than was possible for their Victorian sisters, and they are less vulnerable to retreat into "neurasthenia."

Mabel Collins Donnelly, in *The American Victorian Woman,* has given us a unique and penetrating insight into the world of these women. She details the struggles of women who faced a society that demanded enormous strength, but primarily recognized weakness. Burdened with the inevitability of childbirth and its often disastrous consequences for their lives and health, many women chose the only possible way out—spinsterhood and abstinence. Those who married bore children, and often lost them and their husbands early, if they themselves survived. They frequently faced a limited and even stifling future in their darkened sitting rooms or bedrooms. Some, however, rose up and created, supported, and fought for their rights and lives, and for those of their sisters.

As I read through this captivating book I heard the voice of a physician lecturing in 1905 that "hard study killed sexual desire in women, took away their beauty, brought on hysteria, neurasthenia, dyspepsia, astigmatism and dysmenorrhea." I could see the words of an 1848 textbook on obstetrics: "She [woman] has a head almost too small for the intellect but just big enough for love." I reflected on the poignancy of Charlotte Perkins Gillman's description of her powerlessness, helplessness, and rage in "The Yellow Wallpaper." In that story she captured the moving and tragic experience of one woman who represented many in her era. Donnelly skillfully details, in this complex, penetrating, and scholarly history, the world of these nineteenth-century women.

This lucid and carefully documented account found me surprised, moved, saddened, and reminded of the torturous road ahead. Myth and stereotype continue to profoundly affect women's lives. As the Red Queen said in *Alice in Wonderland,* it will take "all the running you can do to keep in the same place. If you want to get somewhere else you must run at least twice as fast as that!"

Carol C. Nadelson, M.D.

ACKNOWLEDGMENTS

Years go into the preparation and writing of a book. I give my thanks to the directors and curators of the fine libraries and archives I have consulted most frequently.

I want to thank Joseph S. Van Why, Director of the Stowe-Day Foundation, Hartford, Connecticut, for permission to quote manuscript material, and the staff of the Stowe-Day Library, particularly Diana Royce and William Staples. I wish also to thank Helen R. Lansberg, Director of the Ruth B. P. Burlingame Research Library of The Institute of Living, Hartford, Connecticut; Christopher Bickford, Director of the Connecticut Historical Society; Jeffrey M. Kaimowitz, Director, and Margaret F. Sax, Associate Curator, of the Watkinson Library, Trinity College, Hartford, Connecticut; Beverley J. Manning, University Librarian III, University of Connecticut Library.

Yvonne Y. Haddad of the Hartford Seminary, and the late John M. Ganter, former Director of Hartford Neighborhood Centers, were also helpful. I am grateful to the late Howard Mumford Jones and to The American Council of Learned Societies for support in the past.

I have benefited from invitations to lecture before groups interested in the cultural patterns from which their grandparents, great-grandparents, and indeed they themselves have emerged. And it was with classes of undergraduate students that I first encountered the excitement generated by the "fiction" of some American nineteenth-century writers on interactions within Victorian families.

I express my appreciation to Jean M. Blase for her deep interest in the Victorians and for the preparation of the typescript; to Doris J. Dzialo for her unfailing courtesy and enthusiasm; to Elizabeth A. Yundt for preparation of the typescript of an earlier version; to Deborah C. Johndro for the typescript of the reference materials.

I am happy to acknowledge the encouragement of my husband, John Donnelly, M.D., and of many friends, especially Shirley K. Griffin, Elizabeth M. Barker, Maxine T. Boatner, Marie T. Gill, Ruth M. Knauft, Patricia K. Ritter, Maria Sassi, Carolyn A. Waller, Lillian E. Weld, and Mary S. Zeller.

To J. O. B. for his generous and constant support of an earlier version, I am grateful especially. The dedication and accomplishments in women's studies of Carol C. Nadelson, M.D., are a source of inspiration to researchers.

I wish also to thank Dr. James T. Sabin, Mim Vasan, and Julia Gould Marothy of Greenwood Press.

The American Victorian Woman

1
SCOPE

This is a study of the myths about the American girl and woman in the middle and late nineteenth century. An attempt is made to describe the dynamics of growing up as a female during this period, with the recognition that there were important variations between individuals, even in the same family. Individuals and groups of women are shown in their responses to commonly held assumptions about women.

Male assumptions about the nature and duty of women are found in published pronouncements of physicians, judges, clergy, and other authority figures. Women's views are usually found in letters, journals, and diaries not intended for publication, although some women wrote for publication.

Expressions of their values by women in patriarchal Victorian society clearly were limited by the opportunities available for such expression. Gerda Lerner remarks that black women, for example, are "doubly victimized by scholarly neglect and racist assumptions." Although white abolitionists wrote about black experiences, there are large gaps, particularly during "the transition from rural to urban life."[1] In some states in the middle of the nineteenth century, it was illegal to teach blacks to read and write. Oral accounts, recorded by others, are the principal sources of black consciousness. Sojourner Truth (Isabella Van Wagener), an eloquent black woman who campaigned for the vote, depended upon white women to write down her speeches. She was born a slave in

Ulster County, New York, was freed by state law in 1828, and lived until 1883.

Working-class white women did not carry this burden of illiteracy. By the middle of the century, almost ninety per cent of white women were literate.[2] But working fifty or sixty hours a week in a factory or in a private home as a domestic employee was unlikely to leave much time or energy for the promotion of changes in working conditions, particularly when male workers in factories were hostile. Furthermore, as a report of 1868 states, "Women do not get, in the average, one-fourth the wages men receive."[3] So most working women lived in meager circumstances.

It was rare for a woman who arrived as an immigrant to rise to leadership in reform movements headed by men and usually for the benefit of men. Such an exception was Mary Harris "Mother" Jones, an Irish immigrant who began as a seamstress, helped to organize miners and railworkers, and who declared, " . . . wherever a fight is on against wrong, I am always there."[4]

Rare too were reformers from the rural poor, like Tennessee and Victoria Claflin, two sisters from a family of ten children in Ohio, performers as children in medicine shows, taken from one small town to another. Victoria Claflin bore a child while in her teens, was soon deserted, became an advocate of suffrage for women, an editor of a feminist journal, a stockbroker, a candidate (illegally) for President of the United States, and ultimately a millionaire and resident of England. Her entire name, including married names, was Victoria Claflin Woodhull Martin. Her sister, sometimes known as Tennie C., also went to England to live, after the death of Commodore Cornelius Vanderbilt, the sisters' benefactor, in 1877. She later became Lady Cook.

It is not possible to predict who will attain self-fulfillment, but odds can be considered. Also it is difficult to separate the factors that were against women as a sex rather than against both sexes; obviously poor men endured some of the same hardships that poor women endured. What is needed is documentation of hardships peculiar to women, as well as those shared with men.

It is clear that the lives of middle-class women gave them leisure time which they could use in a variety of ways. In an era in which it is estimated that there was one servant for each 6.6 white families and in which middle-class women were primarily managers of the household, nurturers of children, and consumers rather than producers, women were able to make varied decisions about the use of their leisure time.[5] They produced some good works, they attended lectures on many subjects—Margaret Fuller's lectures were well attended in Boston, and the lecture halls of most cities were full of matrons and younger women. They spent immense amounts of time embroidering. "An embroidered tombstone" is the name Catharine Beecher gave to the popular mourning piece.[6] Younger women also spent many hours doing amateur watercolors and planning parties for both good causes and no causes.

It is estimated that by 1896 about one hundred thousand women were affiliated with clubs and social organizations, most of them middle class in membership, others, probably few, working class.[7] Throughout the century, women constituted the majority of churchgoers and workers for temperance, and, earlier in the century, for suffrage for blacks. Was this participation a carrying-out of the prevailing ideal of womanhood for the century, as expressed by many men, and by such conservative women as Catharine Beecher, that "Woman . . . is the chief minister of the family estate in the Christian family?"[8]

There is no doubt that such a prosperous woman as Mrs. Samuel Colt, widow of the munitions king, wanted to do a good work when she helped found a settlement house for the poor, especially women, in the city of Hartford, Connecticut, in 1872. She also found it pleasant to engage in the social activities that accompanied fund-raising for good causes. Mrs. Colt was the daughter of a clergyman, and surely it felt good to her to do good, while at the same time her handsome home was a mansion and her jewelry a conversation piece. She was sufficiently moved by the plight of the poor to help found a neighborhood center and a reading room, yet one cannot imagine her visiting the hovels that Elizabeth Cady Stanton visited and afterwards working for political and social reforms. Nor can one imagine her on the lecture circuit on a chilly night in Kansas, along with Stanton and Susan B. Anthony.

In short, if a sense of *sisterly* affection existed, as contrasted with a sense of helping the poor as part of religious upbringing, it can be discovered principally in the letters and journals of individual women. Whatever the motive, good works were needed; without the settlement houses and alms-houses and "Societies for Social Welfare" founded by the prosperous, the plight of the Victorian poor would have been worse than it was. The thinking of many of the founders, however, did not necessarily include wishes for changing the political and social status of the less powerful. It was the work of a small number of women that late in the century led to the vote for women in several Western states and to reforming divorce and property laws. It should also be said that men, as well as women, were active in reforms for the underprivileged, including women, although it is also a fact that such male reformers as Henry Stanton and Horace Greeley wavered on many occasions and sometimes rejected reforms proposed by women colleagues.

Nor can temperament be overlooked. Within the Victorian family, as in the family today, the values of children often varied widely. Stellar examples of variation are Catharine Beecher and Isabella Beecher Hooker, sister and half-sister of the better-known Harriet Beecher Stowe. Catharine felt that the status of women already was noble and that the vote would degrade her, whereas Isabella worked for woman suffrage.

Economic class considered in terms of yearly income is not a sufficient prognosticator of the self-image and behavior of women. For example, the Beecher sisters belonged to the genteel poor. Daughters of a minister, they were obliged to work as teachers while still in their teens. Although they earned no more than some factory workers, they were well-read, came from a respected family, and took themselves seriously as important people in the community. Later there grew in Catharine a great sadness, and in Isabella a great rage, from their father's decision to send only his sons on to higher education;

but the pride of the sisters remained rooted in their sense of gentility.

Pride in one's abilities was not always enough to sustain during a crisis; certainly it was not enough for Harriet Beecher Stowe when her budding literary efforts were interrupted by the arrival of several children in a very few years. She became severely depressed, suffered from hysterical blindness, and left her husband and children in Cincinnati while she traveled East and stayed in a rest home of quality for almost a year.

There is no doubt, however, that Harriet was fortunate in being financially able to go to a good sanitarium in order to recover from her clinical depression. The very poor, by contrast, when they had serious emotional illness were likely to be sent to a large hospital, like the one on Blackwell's Island in New York, where they were roped together during their afternoon walks, to prevent their escape and possible drowning.[9]

It must always be remembered, however, that even the very poor, like sharecroppers, sometimes had emotional resources that eased hardships. In the sharecropping system many a black mother was able to divide her time between home and fields as she judged necessary.

The frequency of stressful events endured by an individual, as well as the intensity of them, must be considered along with economic circumstances. The Beecher sisters provide once again remarkable material. After Harriet Beecher Stowe published the immensely popular *Uncle Tom's Cabin*, in 1852, her headaches disappeared, headaches she had carried with her from Ohio to Maine. Clearly her success compensated for her stresses. Catharine Beecher, on the other hand, who had rationalized that she didn't need the higher education offered to her brothers but not to her, was rejected by editors when she sent them her serious writings on religion: academic credentials would have helped her. She turned to writing on household management and appeared to be proud of it, but her modest success in the face of her sister's blossoming reputation was not enough for her. She eventually became a depressed woman living in genteel poverty.

Although opportunities for women were much more limited than those available to men, white women had more opportunity in the nineteenth century to expand their consciousness than ever they had had before. In 1850, some eighty-seven per cent of white women over age twenty were literate, and with the cheap printing made possible by the Industrial Revolution, there appeared inexpensive newspapers, magazines, and books that aired matters of particular interest to women.[10] In the 1870's, for a dime a woman could buy *Woodhull and Claflin's Weekly*, a radical feminist journal. And far away from New York, in Kansas, *Lucifer*—a radical feminist journal—sprang up, edited by Moses Harmon. To this journal, exhausted farm women, worn out from frequent pregnancies and almost despairing of relief, confided their fears, and from it they received advice.

Conservative newspapers were in the majority, but they unwittingly served to raise the consciousness of women as the coverage of features and news items grew larger. For example, the Hartford, Connecticut *Courant*, a capital city newspaper, reported on May 10, 1889 the speech of a suffragist from Albany to the Connecticut General Assembly. The all-male Assembly listened to her during their lunch break, in order not to interrupt their real business. She declared: "We ask for the ballot because we don't like the company we are in—with the Indians, paupers, idiots, and criminals (although I have seen many idiots voting)." Most thoughtful women readers must have realized the irony that after years of campaigning for the vote for blacks, women still were without suffrage.

There are two opposite scenarios about the status of American Victorian women, and each of them appears valid until the documentation on the other side is examined. On the one hand, women were dominated by men, not permitted to vote, and were losers in most property and divorce actions. They suffered from a variety of psychosomatic ailments, sometimes labeled as "neurasthenia." A survey by Catharine Beecher of her friends and acquaintances in almost two hundred towns in the Free States found only one married woman in ten regarded as healthy by her middle-class peers. A major disability cited was "pelvic disorder."[11]

On the other hand, Dr. Clelia Mosher, in her survey of middle-class women, most of them graduates of college or normal school, reported that over a third of her forty-five respondents were in good health and reached orgasm "always" or "usually."[12] And Peter Gay, in a close examination of the journals of Mabel Loomis Todd of Andover, Massachusetts, reveals a middle-class Victorian woman of strong sensual appetite.[13] (She also had a husband who not only accepted her longlasting affair with Austin Dickinson, brother of the poet, but who also encouraged it.) Nor were less sophisticated Victorians necessarily less sensual. The diary of Lester Frank Ward of rural Eastern Pennsylvania in 1861 contains many entries about the *mutual* pleasures of lovemaking: "I kissed her on her sweet breasts, and took too many liberties with her sweet person, and we are going to stop."[14]

Mavericks, whether in sexual behavior, political activity, or any one of the social activities available, existed in Victorian times as they do now. Yet, for the majority of women, male dominance was a fact of life. Carl Degler reports that in 1872–1876 some sixty-three per cent of all divorces granted to women were for "grounds that implied inadequate or inappropriate familial behavior by husbands. The general grounds were cruelty, desertion, drunkenness, and neglect to provide." An accompanying fact is that "over 80 per cent of the grounds cited by husbands" during the same period "concerned wives' failures to live up to a submissive subordinant."[15] In a Hartford, Connecticut newspaper, there was published an account from the *Atlanta Constitution* of a man arrested for whipping his wife. The justice of the peace dismissed the charge because the beating was administered with the left hand![16] Elizabeth Packard of Illinois was committed by her husband to a state mental hospital because she disagreed with his religious views.[17]

It was quite possible for a woman to be brave and adventurous, to go with her family in a wagon train to the West, to face the hardships and dangers that went with the trek, and

yet to carry with her a copy of *Godey's Lady's Book*, both for
news about fashion and for advice to emigrants.[18] The Western wife, says Julie Roy Jeffrey in her study of frontier women,
was "both masculine and feminine at the same time."[19] The
typical Western wife was not like Calamity Jane, but instead
carried her East Coast conservatism with her.

The number of sources for the lives of American Victorian
women is impressive. Theirs was the beginning of the age of
surveys: there are surveys of prostitutes, factory women, and
middle-class women at home. There are journals of city women
and farm women and letters of many moods. And there is the
creative writing by both men and women that also explores
relationships between the sexes.

This study of Victorian sexual politics includes both mavericks and conventional women from different backgrounds,
in private and in public life. They have in common that they
were not treated as full citizens. Furthermore, although biology was not destiny for all of them, the consensus was, from
childhood onwards, that the female body was a vulnerable one,
and from biological vulnerability there was assumed vulnerability in general. The possibility of pregnancy, whether within
wedlock or outside it, whether the result of consent, rape, in-
cest, or prostitution, was a major factor in women's lives.
Pregnancy was sometimes viewed as glorious—a popular title
was "The Glory of Woman"—but it was often viewed with the
fear of its ending in puerperal fever or dangerous abortion.

As medical technology improved, with knowledge of antisepsis and the invention of anesthesia, risk began to lessen,
but Victorian knowledge about the female reproductive system remained limited. Their knowledge about women's fertility cycle was, in fact, erroneous.

It is not surprising that a large number of Victorian women
chose not to marry. Yet single or married, they depended upon
father or husband, and in the case of the factory worker, upon
the male employer. The women factory worker worked for fifty-
five or sixty hours a week, as her male co-workers did, but
she worked for lower wages than a man received for the same
job. If she was a servant, and seventy per cent of women
workers in 1870 were domestics, she received a dollar or two

a week and room and board. A black woman earned even less.[20]

It is clear that there were differences in goals and behavior among American Victorian women. However, most of them had been subject to a system intended to produce compliant beings. The sphere of females was understood to be separate and different from that of males and subject to the patriarchal system. The expectation of protection with domination under father's roof was carried to protection with domination under husband's roof. The message was to comply or be punished, in ways subtle or brutal. The methods that encouraged compliance began in childhood.

2

GOOD GIRLS

Conditioning of females to be docile began early. In the nineteenth century, as in some places in the twentieth, the double standard existed even for children. Little girls were expected to be good; little boys, although exhorted to improve themselves, were expected to do daring, questing things. Little girls were occasionally shown as silly and vain, but they were also neat and non-violent. Little boys, however, pulled wings off insects, played with matches, and were slovenly at the table.

The Juvenile Miscellany (*JM*), a magazine published in Boston, assumed that most of its readers would be girls, and it taught proper behavior for girls. A typical story is "Happiness, or Ruth Brook." This is the tale of a girl who is "her father's crowning blessing, and her mother's pearl of price."[1] Ruth becomes orphaned, lodges for a while with the village schoolteacher, "a nice, kind, prim good woman" (what other kind of woman would have been selected to teach school?), and is finally chosen for adoption. Ruth lives according to a verse reprinted in the story.

> Then humbly take what God bestows
> And like his own fair flowers
> Look up in sunshine with a smile
> And gently bend in showers.[2]

The message is to submit, and the protagonist is a girl. The verse reinforces the moral of the opening paragraph of the story that "the great art of life is to make circumstances contribute to happiness, and not happiness dependent on circumstances."

Another story in the collection, "Lucy and Her Monkey," is about not a good, but a spoiled, little girl, although her mother shows good sense.[3] Impulsively Lucy decides to adopt a monkey, Jocco, the pet of the washer-woman's child. Once in the household, Jocco does impulsive and bad things, as Lucy's sensible mother predicts he will do, for he is only an animal. Clearly Jocco's behavior is going to provide a lesson for Lucy!

There is suspense as the reader wonders what new horrors the monkey will commit; there is also a sermon by Lucy's mother about the differences between animals and human beings. (Most of the stories provide the pleasure of plot and the preaching of a moral.)

> I will tell you, my dear—God has given men, women, and children reason and intelligence—when they show any marks of these powers, we are not surprised—but to animals he has given only instinct, that is, a desire of what they want, and the means of attaining it—and to some the power of imitating men and women. Now Jocco belongs to a race that have this last gift in a surprising degree. But you must remember it is only our least valuable gifts that he imitates—he cannot learn to read or write, he cannot be taught that God is his creator.[4]

Jocco, confined to Lucy's bedroom, shreds her beautiful quilt, but his extreme destructiveness is saved for the last page, which reads like a juvenile version of Poe's *Murders in the Rue Morgue*. Instead of a human body jammed up the chimney by an ape, Lucy's elegant wax doll is shoved up the chimney by the monkey. "The soot came tumbling down and with it the elegant wax doll—alas, how changed; its eyes picked out, its face broken, its beautiful white silk dress covered with ashes and soot."

Inconsolable, Lucy weeps: "I never shall want a companion again that has no soul." In real life Lucy might have grown up to be an idealist, like Isabella Beecher of Hartford, Connecticut, who wrote to her fiancé, John Hooker, "I acknowledge great cause for thankfulness—that you dear Sir—are one—to whom I can in all love render the required obedience without being constantly reminded that such is the will of God & the expectation of man—I don't know how it can be otherwise than galling to a sensible woman. . . . "[5] In her later years, Isabella developed mixed feelings about her marriage.

Can one imagine an American story for a *boy* that would have him express his desire for companionship with someone with a "soul," someone to whom he can render the "required obedience?" It is unimaginable that a letter with such timid sentiments as Isabella Hooker's could have been written by a *man* to his betrothed.

In Lucy's room, incidentally, there is a dollhouse that reproduces on a small scale the prosperous house in which Lucy lives. It comes complete with "Cuffee and Dinah, two nice-looking domestics with black bead eyes, faces as black as coal, lips as red as cherries, and teeth as white as ivory." (The black servant was not a rarity in a typical Northern town. In New Haven, for example, by 1820, blacks, slave and free, made up almost five per cent of the population.) Lucy is being trained as a manager of domestic help.

Home and the family are glorified for the girl reader of *JM*. In "An Agreeable Surprise," the father of the family is to be given a surprise birthday party and is asked to come home at "an early hour."[6] (Since he arrives at eight, he presumably has a long day!) He finds the parlor decorated "with flowers and evergreens" and a music box concealed among the plants busy playing "Sweet Home—the dearest, sweetest song of all." The story ends with the traditional moral: "Most happy should be the father of such a family!"

The only selection in the June 1835 issue, which is addressed specifically to a boy, "Dear William," is not written as a story but as a supposed real letter from "Frederick Haskell's Voyage Round the World."[7] The letter, one of a series, is supposedly from Rio de Janeiro, and it comments on the English, on the architecture of a chapel, and on the state of Argentinian blacks ("no better than brutes") contrasted with the state of American blacks in Charleston ("clothed decently, and well treated"). Writing to William, the author says: "I have since seen companies of free blacks, who had as fine an appearance,

and as excellent discipline as any white soldiers I ever
saw. . . . The officers are most of them intelligent men, and
mingle in good society. I have seen negro merchants and negro priests nowise inferior to their white brethren."

The writer of the letter is clearly an intelligent and obser-
vant person writing to a young *man* about *"masculine"* subjects: architecture, the race question, comparative customs. How
much more challenging is this social commentary intended for
boys than the two "domestics" and Lucy's dollhouse intended
for girls! Boys were encouraged to be studious; girls were not.
The Well Bred Boy (1839) has as a frontispiece an engraving
of a boy reading, surrounded by thick volumes and with a globe
of the world on a pedestal near his elbow.[8]

It seems clear that the world of young girls was presented
in domestic terms, rather than as part of the large world of
knowledge and nations. Editor Sarah Buell Hale, an advocate
for better education for women, apparently saw no connection
between the pap she selected for girl readers and the literate
but passive adult females in America.

Even the advertisements for books in *JM* publicize the mar-
tyrdom of females. The advertisement for *The Sunday School
Teacher's Funeral* discloses that the teacher is female (of course)
and that she died happy, although prematurely.

> We dare say you can find it at any of the Bookstores where
> they keep good books for the young; and this one is among the
> best. Do not think it is a melancholy tale. True it is about sick-
> ness, and death, but these are events that *will* happen to all—
> they need not be melancholy. It is the manner in which a per-
> son meets death, that makes it happy or miserable:—and Rachel
> Benson died so happy that you will feel there is pleasure in
> leaving this world when one has a sure hope of going to heaven.[9]

Obviously both men and women died, but the favorite victims in literature of the nineteenth century are females: Harriet Stowe's Eva and Dicken's Little Nell are well-known victims. Henry James allows a young boy to die, as sensitive as
any girl victim, in *The Pupil*, but the female victim is his favorite. In real life the death that most fascinated James was
the death of his girl cousin, from tuberculosis. He sought from

his mother all the details about her dying, even to the appearance of the corpse. *The Wings of The Dove* is probably James's finest elegy for a loved and gracious woman; Kate, the aggressive female in the novel, is, on the other hand, a liar and a cheat. The generous woman, dead, is noble, whereas the shrewd female survivor will always be unhappy.

It was assumed that the female nature was finer, more delicate, than the male. Writers on etiquette ordered the male to pick up a fallen handkerchief and do all manner of small niceties. In turn, the female had a greater burden of graciousness: child or adult, she was supposed to die with elegance and to endure dying graciously. Stowe's Eva on her deathbed, and Finley's Elsie Dinsmore on hers, are models of patience and zeal to reform their erring fathers. Elsie recovers from brain fever, and her father is born again to a better life. Eva's father too becomes a better person, although her mother remains as selfish as ever. The creators of these characters, in addition to knowing that a weeping reader is a loyal reader, believed that a good life which serves as a model for others is worthwhile, even if death comes early. But females die most beautifully of all.

It is fair to add that Harriet Stowe did not say that all good people should be good victims. She created not only Eva, but also Eliza, who fled bondage and took risks to secure her freedom. Yet the unpleasant question remains: Why are there so many *female* victims in nineteenth-century literature? Tuberculosis, for example, "consumption" as it was called, was clearly not a *female* disease! Yet the "Ode to Sickness," in a book of readings for elocutionists, is noted by the editor to have been written by "a young lady . . . who for many years had been oppressed with a hopeless consumption." Of course, a young *lady*! The poem begins:

> Not to the rosy maid, whom former hours
> Beheld me fondly covet, tune I now
> The melancholy lyre: no more I seek
> Thy aid, Hygeia! sought so long in vain;
> But 'tis to *thee*, O Sickness! 'tis to thee
> I wake the silent strings; accept the lay.[10]

With a rather clumsy syntax, the poem announces the acceptance of sickness instead of health, pallor instead of rosiness. The poem breathes the pathos of terminal illness and it comes from a woman, not a man. The highest duty of a female, according to Victorians, was to suffer.

In a Victorian book with colored pictures, *Struwwelpeter*, written in 1845 by a German physician, the contrast between boys and girls is strongly made.[11] The book is dedicated to both boys and girls and contains rhymed stories illustrated in garish colors about nine bad children. Only one of them, Harriet (boy's name variant), is a girl. She plays with matches and sets herself afire, leaving only her red shoes in the ashes.

She is the only bad female among the many bad boys. The boys sometimes come to a bad end, but usually the girls are perfect. Boys are exhorted to be manly. Little Suck-a-thumb, for example, is pounced on by a hideous tailor who cuts off his offending fingers with a giant scissors.

> Snip! Snap! Snip! the scissors go,
> And Conrad cries out "Oh! Oh! Oh!"
> Snip! Snap! Snip! They go so fast,
> That both his thumbs are off at last.
> Mamma comes home: there Conrad stands,
> And looks quite sad, and shows his hands,
> "Ah!" said Mamma, "I knew he'd come
> To naughty little Suck-a-thumb."[12]

So Conrad is taught brutally to avoid such babyish behavior as thumbsucking. As for Conrad's mother, she is a stern matron who wastes no tears on her son. He is expected to be manly. If he develops a castration complex, she will take no blame for it! And, of course, most tactile pleasures, masturbation most of all, were a matter of concern throughout the nineteenth century. Inquiring fingers were dealt with brutally in real life.

Punishments for children varied with the bias of the parents. Such a traveler as Alexis de Tocqueville, after visiting the United States, contrasted the informality and aggressive behavior of American children with the more subdued behavior of European children.[13] Doubtless behavior varied with social class as much as with nation. In the United States, a carefully reared child was expected to behave with moderation, and middle-class Catharine Beecher and other writers on household management usually included a chapter on the importance of good manners in children. But among the urban poor (by 1880 twenty per cent of the population lived in cities) violence flared in children as well as in adults. Stephen Crane in *Maggie* (1893) describes a father in a slum of New York City who comes upon his son, Jimmie, after the boy has been in a neighborhood fight. "Jimmie arose painfully from the ground and, confronting his father, began to curse him. His parent kicked him. 'Come home now,' he cried, 'an stop yer jawin' er I'll lam the everlasting head off yehs.' "[14]

Jimmie, being male, in time inherits his father's authority in the family. "He stumbled upstairs late at night, as his father had done before him. He reeled about the room, swearing at his relations, or went to sleep on the floor."

For his sister, Maggie, however, to be female is to be dominated and beaten, first by her father and mother (mother is as much a beast as father), then by her brother. Finally, she becomes a sex object for a man who says, "Mag, I'm stuck on yer shape. It's outa sight." (This was daring for a popular story in Victorian times.) Jilted by her man, Maggie finally commits suicide.

Out West, Huckleberry Finn at first glance seems to be making a joyful escape from the world of genteel women, pious ladies who make him wash himself and attend Sunday School and give up smoking. So when his father forces him to leave the widow and live in a riverside cabin, at first he enjoys the change.

It was kind of lazy and jolly, laying off comfortable all day, smoking and fishing, and no books nor study. Two months or more run along, and my clothes got to be all rags and dirt, and I didn't see how I'd ever got to like it so well as the widow's, where you had to wash, and eat on a plate, and comb up, and go to bed and get up regular, and be forever bothering over a book. . . . It was pretty good times up in the woods there, take it all around.[15]

Good times, no responsibility, no nagging genteel women. "But by-and-by pap got too handy with his hick'ry and I couldn't stand it. I was all over welts." After being locked in and terrorized by his drunken father, Huck manages to saw his way out of the cabin. As he travels along the river on a raft, he is gentled by a runaway slave, Jim, who is no boy, but a husband and father, although Twain minimizes these facts. At first Huck is cruel to Jim by pretending that Jim has only dreamed, not experienced, Huck's disappearance in a canoe. But confronted with Jim's misery at being tricked, Huck apologizes, and Jim says, "trash is what people is dat puts dirt on de head er day fren's en makes 'em ashamed." Humbled, Huck shows a sense of fair play. He is gentled, and by one of life's losers, as the majority would have viewed Jim. Jim acts like a nurturing woman.

In nightmarish chapter eighteen, Huck flees to Jim as he would to a woman, for comfort. He has just experienced the horrors of a feud being acted out.

> All of a sudden, bang! bang! bang! goes three or four guns—the men had slipped around through the woods and come in from behind without their horses! The boys jumped for the river— both of them hurt—and as they swum down the current the men run along the bank shooting at them and singing out, "Kill them, kill them!" It made me so sick I most fell out of the tree. I ain't agoing to tell *all* that happened—it would make me sick again if I was to do that. I wished I hadn't ever come ashore that night to see such things . . . lots of times I dream about them.[16]

As Huck runs along the river bank looking for the raft and safety, he hears Jim's voice: "Lawsy, I's mighty glad to git you back again, honey."

White males do not address each other as "Honey," but black Jim can use the word and Huck as a boy is allowed to take comfort in it. Similarly Ishmael in Melville's *Moby-Dick* entwines his limbs, accidentally, during sleep in a shared double bed with a man of color; or perhaps the man of color, a tatooed Polynesian, does the entwining. It doesn't matter, because with people who are "different," as with children, the usual taboos do not have to be observed. Again, in the scene when Ishmael's hands touch the hands of other sailors as they squeeze spermaceti lumps back into fluid, he feels ecstasy based upon very physical sensations.

> Squeeze! squeeze! squeeze! all the morning long; I squeezed that sperm till I myself almost melted into it; I squeezed that sperm till a strange sort of insanity came over me; and I found myself unwittingly squeezing my co-laborers' hands in it, mistaking their hands for the gentle globules. Such an abounding, affectionate, friendly, loving feeling did this avocation beget; that at last I was continually squeezing their hands, and looking up into their eyes sentimentally.[17]

How very much male writers had to labor for circumstances in which tender emotions could be displayed in an "acceptable" way! Perhaps the world of male violence, the world of guns and killing, from which Huck Finn fled in favor of the comforting presence of Jim, was a world that many Victorian men really feared. But to face the fact would have been to join the inferior sex, the weak sex, the female sex. And who would want to do that?

Margaret Fuller, who was a teacher, editor, and organizer of women's clubs, declared she had never met a man who wanted to exchange places with a woman. In turn, her brother, when editing her papers after her early death, emphasized in his preface her contributions to the "home," not to the outside world that had been so important to her—"home, where best the *heart* and *soul* can be known."[18]

3

FATHER'S GIRL

After a childhood in which the principal message to a girl was "Submit," the young woman was usually ready to regard father as the power in the household. If mother was self-confident too (and she was more likely to be self-confident if she received attention from the outside world), the daughter had a model of a female both caring and self-assured. But many Victorian mothers either were invalids, or considered themselves invalids, so that a questing daughter was likely to admire father as doer and achiever, and to pity, sometimes even despise, mother as passive and boring.

The admiration of daughter for father need not be considered solely in Freudian terms; unconscious sexual attraction need not be interpreted as the sole basis for dominance. It is readily understandable that a bright and lively young woman would be more excited by father moving in the world of events than by mother dozing on a couch. This is not to say that during such a traumatic episode as giving birth or having a first period, female-to-female bonding was not important; surely it was. But such dissimilar young women as Emily Dickinson and Jane Addams found their father, not their mother, to be the important person in their early lives. Father represented power. An astonishing number of young women remained Daddy's girls in Victorian America, although the title they used was "Father," as with God.

Elsie Dinsmore, Martha Finley's popular young heroine, was

the recipient of more of father's kisses than most girls today would want to receive. A tall, husky man, he is forever stooping "to press a kiss upon the quivering lips."[1] Elsie's goal is to reform her father, and when she is near death (from which she miraculously recovers, or there would have been no best-seller series), he repents and becomes so ideal a father that Elsie later wonders whether any young man will match him. Her mother, of course, is dead—a fact of life in many Victorian households and a fact in many novels—and Elsie is, until she marries, the provider of gentle femininity in the household.

Eva, Harriet Stowe's young heroine, has a living mother, but Eva is portrayed as far superior to mother. Furthermore, father is fonder of Eva than he is of mother. Mother is worthless and selfish, although Eva does her best to be patient. When Eva dies of a consumption that turns her cheeks pale, father has little left in life that he cares about. When *he* dies, however, heartless mother still has, as a Southern woman, the slaves who were part of her dowry, and she does quite well without her husband. Neither father nor daughter, it is clear, was important to her. Nor was she important to them, just as in many Victorian families the bond between father and daughter was much closer than between husband and wife. (It is possible that the high disease and mortality rate among young mothers made father appear to be the stable survivor in the view of the anxious children.)

In the real-life South, one of the closest and most productive relationships between father and daughter was that of Sarah Grimké and her father. He was a wealthy slave owner, and she was the sixth of fourteen children. Her prolific mother is portrayed as a harsh supervisor of the family's slaves. It is clear that father is the one whom Sarah admired. Mother was the cruel parent, the one who did the punishing of both slaves and children, whereas father encouraged Sarah to study and to be his companion. She also nursed him during a long illness. When his illness took him to Philadelphia, she was his devoted nurse-companion. It was after his death in Philadelphia that she joined the Quakers and took an antislavery stand.

Sarah's sister, Angelina, followed a similar path. The death of their father and a beloved brother enabled them to cut their ties to Charleston and their mother.

Letters between Mrs. Mary Grimké and her daughters reveal the degree of alienation between them.[2] The daughters were horrified that their mother not only had refused to free her slaves, but that she rented out a house-slave named Stephen who was then obliged to do heavy work for which he was unsuited. Separated from his wife, who worked in a different household, Stephen lived from time to time in a poorhouse, suffered from epileptic seizures, and finally went North, sponsored by the Grimké sisters. It is not surprising that Lucretia Coffin Mott, a Quaker and a leader among abolitionists and workers for woman suffrage, supplanted Mrs. Grimké as a nurturer of the Grimké daughters.

Up North, in Amherst, Massachusetts, a woman talented in poetry rather than politics also rejected her mother but in a different manner from the Grimkés. Emily Dickinson's mother had been a Norcross, a prosperous family in Western Massachusetts; but as her two daughters, Emily and Vinnie, and her son, Austin, grew up, Mrs. Dickinson spent more and more time propped up on a couch or a chair. The son married but lived next door. The daughters never married. They baked father's favorite breads and cakes and ran his house and the garden.

What was Mrs. Dickinson's illness? She was often troubled with toothache and went about with a swollen jaw that made her self-conscious, but her problems were more serious than these. Emily wrote in 1856 when her mother was fifty-two: "mother lies upon the lounge or sits in her easy chair. I don't know what her sickness is, for I am but a simple child. . . ."[3] The "simple child" was then twenty-six, hardly a schoolgirl. Perhaps Mrs. Dickinson was suffering from what Victorians delicately called "pelvic disorder." (This was one of the favorite complaints of the married women surveyed by Catharine Beecher in a sample from almost two hundred towns.) In any case, that year Mrs. Dickinson went to a water-cure establishment in Northampton, not far from her home, where presumably she was treated sympathetically, surrounded by other women like herself. But she did not improve.

Emily became increasingly important to her father. She wrote in 1858: "I do not go out at all, lest Father will come and miss me, or miss some little act, which I might forget, should I run away—Mother is much as usual—I know not what to hope of her."[4] When middle-aged wives cracked like brittle teacups, young daughters took over the kitchen, the house, and father. As Emily wrote,

> Like a Cup—
> Discarded of the Housewife-
> Quaint- or Broken-
> A newer Sevres pleases-
> Old Ones crack-[5]

And so, in addition to writing poems in the quiet of her room, Emily baked bread and cake, ran errands, and admired the distinguished visitors who came to talk with her distinguished father, while her undistinguished mother vegetated on the couch or in bed.

In 1863, Mother seemed ludicrous to Emily, Mother with her swollen jaw, who looked like a baby cutting teeth. Wrote Emily, "Teething didn't agree with her, and she kept her bed, Sunday, with a face that would take a premium at any cattle-show in the land."[6] Mrs. Dickinson's face, bulging because of infected teeth and ill-fitted dentures, probably looked ugly—ridiculous too—but the remark is nasty as well as humorous.

Certainly Emily did her duty when her mother became paralyzed, but more than ever her mother was in a passive position, the position in which Emily perceived her always. She wrote soon after her mother's death, "We were never intimate Mother and Children while she was our Mother—but Mines in the same Ground meet by tunneling and when she became our Child the Affection came—"[7] The affection came when the child-mother who had had "teething" problems was dead.

On the one hand, after her mother's death in 1882, Emily seems detached; mother in the grave is a "picture." "Mother was very beautiful when she had died. . . . The illumination that comes but once paused upon her features, and it seemed like hiding a picture to lay her in the grave."[8]

Yet in another letter written near the same time, soon after her mother's death, Emily refers to her mother's "dear eyes . . . dear face."[9] It was a "dear face," but also, as she said in a letter to Otis P. Lord, to whom she would have spoken from the heart, a "timid face."[10] Mrs. Norcross could not have served as a model for Emily; she could only have been a pitiable figure, a lost, timid child.

Yet, in a study based upon the correspondence and diaries of women in thirty-five families between the 1760's and 1860's, Carroll Smith-Rosenberg finds an absence of that hostility between mothers and daughters which is regarded today as a usual stage in the development of young women. Smith-Rosenberg ascribes to "the extended female network" based upon the many female relationships that flourished in the Victorian extended family, boarding schools, and the like, a means of displacement of hostility between mother and daughter.[11] Certainly the relationships between females were many and tender, but it also seems likely that in many families that contained talented young women like Dickinson and Jane Addams, mother was viewed as so passive and powerless that she was not likely to be taken seriously as a rival.

Emily Dickinson's letters show how important to her for many years were the friendships that began in her schoolgirl days. Not only were her relationships with her sister and sister-in-law important to her, but also relationships with friends such as Jane Humphrey. Jane lived with the Dickinsons when Emily was twelve and shared a bedroom, and probably a bed, with her. Certainly today's middle-class goal of one child to one bedroom was neither desired nor likely in Victorian households.

Emily wrote to Jane on May 12, 1842, "What good times we used to have jumping into bed when you slept with me,"[12] and she wrote to Jane until 1855, when she was thirty-five. The letters contain the intimate and concrete language of affection that Smith-Rosenberg also finds among the women she studied.

In April 1850, Jane was away teaching, and Emily wrote longingly: "I have wished, and prayed to *see* you, and to *hear* you, and to feel your warm heart beating near me, what music in such quiet ticking."[13] She continues in the same letter, "I shall see you *sometime* darling. . . . " Later, in April of 1852, when she was preoccupied with the thought of becoming "old and gray" (although she was only thirty-two), she wrote, "sometimes think of me, and how dearly I loved you, and love you still."[14]

The last known letter to Jane, written in 1855, shows love and regret. "How I wish you were mine, as you once were, when I had you in the morning, and when the sun went down, and was sure I should never go to sleep without a moment from you."[15]

The language is the language of love, but this is not to imply that there was any acting out of the feeling in an explicitly sexual way. Such inferences are made hastily today about contemporaries, but the fact is that Jane and Emily as adults seldom saw each other, for Jane was away teaching in Ohio and elsewhere. The point is that intimate friendship between Victorian women was accompanied by letters of much warmth, whereas the letters between a well-bred man and woman, even during their engagement, tended to be rather formal. For example, Isabella Beecher, writing to her fiancé, John Hooker, shows cordial and respectful feeling rather than passionate or even warm feeling.[16]

It cannot be assumed, however, that there was less rivalry between sisters, or even between some friends, than there is now. Catharine Beecher, writing to her sister, Mary Beecher Perkins, for example, in 1837, shows some patronizing when she refers to her sister, Harriet, as "poor thing," worn out already from two babies and another on the way.[17]

But the loyalty of daughters to father, even when they recognized his favoritism toward his sons, was powerful, no matter the hurt. Father was king. Aging queens often became invalids, but there were many eager princesses.

It was not only such impoverished daughters as Catharine Beecher who exalted father. Jane Addams, rich enough to travel abroad and finally to establish her own settlement house in Chicago, demonstrates in her reminiscences the strong attraction her father held for her.

She writes vividly of an event when she was twelve, in 1872.

Giuseppe Mazzini, the great Italian liberator and worker for Italian unification, had just died, and Jane's father, stirred to eloquence, recounted to his young daughter Mazzini's great achievements. Jane as an adult recalled:

> I obtained that which I have ever regarded as a valuable possession, a sense of the genuine relationship which may exist between men who share large hopes and like desires, even though they differ in nationality, language, and creed; that these things count for absolutely nothing between groups of men who are trying to abolish slavery in America or to throw off Hapsburg oppression in Italy.[18]

Note that Jane refers to "men," not "people."

It was her father to whom important people came in Jane's childhood. These occasions were " . . . red-letter days, when a certain general came to see my father." Her father was for sixteen years a member of the state senate, and she recalled, "Even as a little child I was dimly conscious of the grave march of public affairs in his comings and goings at the state capital."

"The grave march of public affairs," the world of power and significance, the male world, which Jane was determined to enter. An eighth child, frail, plagued by curvature of the spine, Jane dealt aggressively with her infirmity, although she spent one spring in Dr. Weir Mitchell's hospital in Philadelphia. She traveled in Europe while she convalesced, learning about settlement work in London, and finally in 1889 purchased the large house in Chicago which would offer room, board, clinics, and the teaching of skills to the immigrant poor. Jane never married. She worked as a powerful figure to effect social change, using her father's money to begin. She achieved recognition, although ironically in a nurturing role, as a leader in the settlement house movement.

Emily Dickinson was a secluded genius; Jane Addams was an aggressive reformer. For both, the key figure was father. Elizabeth Cady Stanton, a major figure in the woman suffrage movement, was by contrast a person willing and able to fill the usual Victorian role of dutiful daughter and later dutiful wife and mother, but to this she added strong achievement in the public arena. In addition, she was able to form a realistic impression of her father.

Stanton is a splendid example of the flourishing of good sense and self-esteem in the face of what was major rejection by her father during her childhood. But the woman, aged eighty-three, reminiscing in 1898 still remembered the wounds of the girl.

The traumatic early events that changed the current of her life were the death of her only brother, her attempt to replace him in her father's affection, and her father's refusal to accept her triumphs as being as important as a son's would have been. The early events remained vivid in her memory. Her brother, the only son in a family of five daughters, died after being graduated from college. Her father was inconsolable. The body lay in state in a casket in the parlor, and eleven-year-old Elizabeth went into the darkened room. The casket was draped in white. The furniture was draped in white. She sat upon her father's knee, hoping to comfort him, hoping he would make her feel essential to him. Instead he sighed and said, "Oh, my daughter, I wish you were a boy!"[19]

She was determined to be at the head of her classes and "thus delight my father's heart." She decided that to equal a boy she must be "learned and courageous." So she began to study Greek and to ride on horseback. Both the intellectual and the physical would be her realms. Meanwhile she also kept her father company through the entire winter, each time he wept at the grave of his son. Always she reminded herself that by means of her accomplishments she would make up for the loss her father felt.

Finally one day, having studied hard for many months, she received a prize at school. She described her expectations: "I ran down the hill, rushed breathless into his office, laid the new Greek Testament, which was my prize, on his table. . . ." His response, uttered with a sigh, was, "Ah, you should have been a boy!"[20]

The event was traumatic in that it was forever deeply felt, yet she remained ambitious. She went on to Emma Willard's Female Academy in Troy, New York, and later appreciated the generosity of her father, who helped a household that eventually included seven children. But she never forgot his disappointment in her.

Her marriage at the beginning was a relatively happy one, for Henry Stanton as an abolitionist understood what it was to be a rebel and to take a minority position. In 1843 he was admitted to the bar and practiced law in Boston. Here Elizabeth met distinguished men, among them Hawthorne, Whittier, Emerson, and William Lloyd Garrison. Here too she met distinguished women who had taken positions against slavery and who were giving lectures on abolition—Lydia Maria Child, Abby Kelley (later Abby Kelley Foster), Paulina Wright Davis, and Maria Chapman.

It was in London, however, soon after her wedding, during an international antislavery convention that Elizabeth was required to sit in a segregated section for women, and it was then that her anger against discrimination according to sex grew strong. It was there that she came to know Lucretia Mott, the Quaker abolitionist.

In 1848 the couple moved to Seneca Falls, New York, "a malarial region," where Elizabeth was lonely and discussed the feeding of infants with Theodore and Angelina Grimké-Weld![21] There "Fourier's phalansterie community life and co-operative households had a new significance for me."[22] Later, "In a tempest-tossed condition of mind," she talked of her discontent with Lucretia Mott and others.[23] "My discontent, according to Emerson, must have been healthy, for it moved us all to prompt action, and we decided, then and there, to call a Woman's Rights Convention."[24] Note that Elizabeth Stanton regarded her discontent as healthy, not worrisome.

One of the saddest examples of an undervalued and often melancholy daughter is Catharine Beecher. She experienced neither the success of her sister, Harriet, nor the rebellion of her half-sister, Isabella. Talented, she would have liked to go to college. Furthermore, her fiancé died at sea; she grieved, and never married.

She wrote about theological matters, but her essays were not taken seriously, and without the endorsement of a college or a seminary, they were regarded as amateurish and even bizarre. At the age of twenty-three, she established an academy for girl students in Hartford, Connecticut, at which her younger sister, Harriet, assisted. The academy was modestly successful, and Catharine lived at home, paying for room and board, and sharing the home with the children of her father's first and second marriages. When he went to Cincinnati to become president of Lane Theological Seminary, Catharine, then thirty-two, joined him. There she established another school for girls, but this one was not successful and eventually failed.

Catharine tried to believe that she was as talented, even more talented, than her brothers who had been sent on to college or seminary. "Five of my father's sons were trained in the best colleges, while his daughters all knew little or nothing of the chief branches included in the college courses. And yet the domestic training of the daughters and their more extensive reading, as I view it, made them fully equal to my brothers in intellectual development."[25] But her rationalization was not enough to sustain her; she was often melancholy.

In contrast, Isabella Beecher Hooker, Catharine's half-sister, who married, had a family, and would in the 1860's turn to the women's movement, allowed herself in 1859 to speak bluntly about the favoritism her father had shown his sons.

> At fifteen my dear good father (instigated of course by his new wife) came to me & suggested, that I should begin to teach school now & support myself. I, who had never been to school in earnest, for two years together in my whole life. . . .
> At sixteen & a half, just when my brothers began their mental education, mine was finished—except as life's discipline was added with years. . . . Till twenty-three, their father, poor minister as he was could send them to College & Seminary all six—cost what it might, but never a daughter cost him a hundred dollars a year, after she was sixteen.[26]

Her anger, however, did not compensate for her sense of "littleness" while she was raising her children.[27]

Whether father was loved or hated, and often both emotions were felt at different times, his word was powerful. Although middle-class and working-class women were permitted to choose their spouses, they were likely to choose someone from their own background, so that father was unlikely to play the part of the father in *The Barretts of Wimpole Street*. He didn't need to: compliance usually came readily. Occasionally the values of the bridegroom differed from those of the father-in-law: Isabella Beecher Hooker's father, for example, was a conservative abolitionist, whereas her husband was a radical abolitionist. Both men, however, were abolitionists, and Isabella herself became one as well.

The most comfortable relationship between mother and daughter in American Victorian times seemed to exist when mother and daughter labored together, away from father, for survival. This was frequently the relationship between black women, particularly for the domestic worker who took her daughter with her to work and sometimes found chores for her to do in the household, thus giving the daughter supervised training as well as protection. Such cooperation for survival was also found among both white and black rural women during and after the Civil War, when they had to manage farms without able-bodied men.

A striking example of a mother-daughter team is that of Sarah Beaulieu and her mother in Wisconsin.[28] For March 27, 1865, Sarah recorded, "Did our usual work. In the afternoon yoked up the oxen and drawed logs for firewood then went to sugar bush with Mother. . . . " On April 3, Sarah and another woman "carried in fifty bushels of turnips out of the pit." Later, in the prairie world of Antonia in Willa Cather's *My Antonia*, effective mother-daughter relationships are based upon women cooperating for survival, regardless of minor bickering and tension.

In Mary E. Wilkins Freeman's story, "The Revolt of Mother," the mother determines to move into a decent farmhouse after many years of living in a cramped one. Her farmer-husband has prospered and keeps building bigger and better barns for his animals, but he is deaf to any proposal to give his family better housing. Finally, while he is away on business, Mother decides to move family and furniture into the brand-new barn, more spacious than her home. She is helped to her radical decision by her desire to give her young and frail daughter a more impressive house from which to be married. Freeman's "Mother" is both nurturing and powerful. However, she was not typical, as Freeman herself was later to declare.

In a bitter article in the *Saturday Evening Post* in 1917, Freeman contrasted Mother, the fictitious Sarah Penn, with real women in New England.

> There never was in New England a woman like Mother. If there had been she certainly would not have moved into the palatial barn. . . . She simply would have lacked the nerve. She would also have lacked the imagination. New England women of the period coincided with their husbands in thinking that the sources of wealth should be better housed than the consumers.[29]

A feminist psychologist, Phyllis Chesler, writes that young women often enter matrimony because they are starved emotionally. Such young women have been deprived of nurturing by their mothers, either because the mothers are emotionally unable to give nurturing, or because they make a son rather than a daughter the important child in the family. Furthermore, when young women have not received a "legacy of power and humanity" from their mothers, they turn to their fathers "for physical affection, nurturance, or pleasurable emotional intensity."[30] Later, therefore, they will seek in husbands what they have been denied by mothers.

In Victorian times, young women were in a double bind. Father usually held control of purse strings and property, and, therefore, power, and middle-class mothers were often passive and melancholy, like the women surveyed by Catharine Beecher in 1855. Such women scarcely served as healthy models for questing daughters, and since jobs outside the home were generally not regarded as desirable for middle-class women, unmarried women usually felt obliged to remain at home. The unmarried daughters of Harriet Beecher Stowe, for example, remained at home with their mother until she died at the age of eighty-five. The prevailing assumption was that an unmarried woman should be a compliant and useful companion to her parents. For some daughters, the assumption was a useful excuse for spinsterhood.

In summary, the experiences in childhood and adolescence of young females tended to fortify father as the authority figure within the family. Furthermore, the female body, once it was sexually mature, became a source of anxiety, and sometimes distaste, for its possessor, who once again sought authoritative words from the male establishment.

The contrast between the images of virile, powerful father and ailing, sensitive mother cannot be overstated. To many young girls and adolescents, the capacity of father to beget new lives with a second or third wife (even after mourning the proper one year) must have been traumatic. The Reverend Lyman Beecher, for example, had nine children by his first wife, four by his second wife, and none by his third, who was forty-seven when he married her. His father, David Beecher, had married five times. It is no wonder that many ambitious Victorian women chose to marry late in life, near or after menopause, or chose not to marry at all.

4

"UNWELL"

One of the Victorian beliefs that most harmed the morale of young women was that studiousness damaged health, particularly serious studying done during the menstrual period. The view was popular among general readers: *Eve's Daughters: or Common Sense for Maid, Wife, and Mother* bore on its title page in an edition of 1882 that it was in its tenth thousand. The author, Marion Harland Terhune, a pseudonym for Mary Virginia Terhune, sympathized with the administrative policy of some colleges that "Students in delicate health will not be received."[1] And, ironically, one way to produce delicate health was to do too much studying.

It is known today that the periods of newly menstruating girls are frequently irregular, but in Victorian times regularity was almost a fetish. Irregularity might even be a sign of tuberculosis! Mothers and daughters were instructed to examine the color of the menses. The color, said physicians, should be bright red, "in appearance and very much like blood from a recently cut finger."[2] One can imagine the association of a cut finger with menstrual blood; no wonder there was so much hysteria among Victorian women. On the other hand, bright red in the sputum was a danger sign. Many a Victorian woman must have examined her assorted discharges several times a week.

Most physicians took a strong stand against intense studying by young women, particularly during the menstrual period. Dr. Edward H. Clarke was shocked at the many cases of amenorrhea, and proclaimed that many women "graduated from school or college excellent scholars but with undeveloped ovaries."[3] He subtitled his book *A Fair Chance for the Girls*, but he was not really interested in a fair chance at all unless the girls gave up scholarly ambition.

The most savage medical diatribe of the time against women was *The Dangers and the Duty of the Hour*, by Dr. William Goodell. He originally presented his views in an address before the "Medical and Chirurgical Faculty of Maryland," but he thought of himself as a speaker "not only as physician to physicians, but as a citizen to citizens, and as a man to men."[4] Clearly not as a person to people. And, of course, technically women were not even full citizens.

He deplored the "pale and sickly" women of his time, their "thin lips and sharp features and those hollow, wistful eyes."[5] He declared vengefully that "another rape of the Sabines" was "possible"—no doubt because the "pale and sickly" women he described did not welcome intercourse![6] "Too much brain-work and too little body-work," he wrote, "is the crying evil in this land. The fact is that our girls are over-educated . . . energy is withdrawn from the trophic and reproductive centres, and physical development is arrested. Precocious cleverness is attainable only at the cost of physical and sexual development."[7]

If Goodell is to be trusted about the rumor, some people even wondered whether there was a plot in boarding schools to prevent monthly periods! "So common indeed it is for girls in boarding schools to suffer from amenorrhea or from irregular menstruation as to create a general impression in the community that, in these schools, some drug is secretly given in the food in order to lessen the laundry work."[8] True that sanitary towels were laundered and reused, but surely Goodell's remark is a paranoid one, and if it was generally held, it implies a goodly amount of sick thinking, not by the young women, but the general community.

What is also distressing is that Dr. Goodell was professor of Clinical and Didactic Gynecology at the University of Pennsylvania, so that he was taken seriously in his views by his colleagues and lay people and in a position in his didactic role to influence medical education. So when he said a woman was literally "unwell" during menstruation, it was something to worry about.

"Unwell"—a word with frightening connotations, a word used into the twentieth century, by the uneducated especially. Nor did Victorian mothers, any more than most Victorian physicians, reassure their daughters. Instead the normal monthly shedding of the endometrium was converted into a horror. *The Glory of Woman* of 1896 was directed toward the ordinary middle-class reader, and it too made menstruation an alarming phenomenon.

> During "the monthly periods," violent exercise is injurious; iced drinks and acid beverages are improper; and bathing in the sea, and bathing in cold water, and cold baths, are dangerous; indeed, at such times as these, no risks should be run, and no experiments should, for one moment, be permitted, otherwise serious consequences will, in all probability, ensue. "The monthly periods" are times not to be trifled with, or woe betide the unfortunate trifler.[9]

What "experiments"? Intercourse perhaps? Masturbation?

With so much woe predicted, it is not surprising that many young women took to sipping cordials and wines and stronger beverages during their periods. Stupor must have been more welcome than feeling fragile. Such tippling was recognized and condemned by the authors of *The Glory of Woman* as "an evil practice"; it was also said to be "very general." The cooperation of mothers who gave their young daughters a sip of cordial to relieve cramps at the time of menstruation was condemned because it was believed to lead the girl "to love spirits."[10] There is no fault in the doctors' logic; anxiety leads to drinking to reduce anxiety. Yet the doctors themselves helped to create the anxiety by their excessive attention to the alleged dangers in normal bodily functions. A further irony is that one of the authors of *Glory* was a woman. Whether she winced at the tendency of her male colleague to invest a normal function with danger cannot be known.

Menstruation was frequently linked to masturbation, and to sexuality in general. It was said that heavy bleeding was brought on by masturbation, a practice that the Victorians feared and condemned. Heavy bleeding was also caused by the use of heated beverages, by daydreams, and even by novel reading! In other words, the slightest stimulation, from hot drinks to masturbation, was believed to encourage profuse bleeding. Sexual fantasies, therefore, were not only immoral, but also they made a woman ill. The authority figure who made these statements was no less than the gynecologist to the Metropolitan Hospital and Dispensary in New York City.[11] From the onset of menstruation then, the young Victorian girl was conditioned to look upon her periods with fear and distaste. The"pelvic organ" was implied to dominate her life and health.

Blood was regarded as fearsome, even the usual spotting and light flow that continues for some days after childbirth. Harriet Beecher Stowe's daughter, Georgiana Stowe Allen, was afraid she would die from hemorrhage, for she mistook the normal discharge after childbirth for a sign of danger. Her anxiety was made worse by the tales of a morbid nursemaid, who chose to regale her with gossip about new mothers who had died in five minutes from postpartum hemorrhage. It was the detective work of Harriet that traced her daughter's anxiety to these tales of the nurse, and it was Harriet's careful ministrations to her daughter, in addition to visits by a physician, that led to Georgie's improvement.[12] However, at this time Georgie was also introduced to painkilling drugs, and to these she developed an addiction.

A woman with time on her hands, and it was presumably such women who read the many manuals about female health, was presented with innumerable opportunities for increased anxiety about her bodily functions. Even the digestive system—a unisex system, after all—was made the object of intense examination. In the back of Catharine Beecher's *Physiology and Calisthenics for Schools and Families* is a section entitled "Water Cure Treatment for Families." Baths and soaks were the rule. For constipation, a frequent complaint, Beecher recommended, in addition to fruit and fiber, "a cold water injection," what today would be called an enema, "after breakfast and on going to bed, the last to be retained, if possible."[13] Vaginal douching was also practiced frequently, for contraception and for cleanliness. Fluids used included tea and milk. It is ironic that although masturbation was feared and severely dealt with, the cold water injection and the douche were widely recommended.

On the other hand, Catharine Beecher and other writers, such as Lydia H. Sigourney, poet and essayist, criticized the prevailing fashion of tight corsets and tight waistbands. (Elaborate gowns with nipped-in waistbands required twenty yards of fabric.) Catharine preferred a "well-fitted jacket to replace stiff corsets."[14] Lydia Huntley Sigourney, in her *Letters to Young Ladies*, chided her readers. "Has it occurred to you, that your own sex . . . has exceeded the ancient stoics in the voluntary infliction of pain, and extinction of pity. . . . They never grappled iron and whalebone into the very nerves and life-blood of their system."[15]

Just as corsets restricted the shape of the body, so the warnings against masturbation restricted the yielding to sexual drive in any but approved circumstances. No warnings were more severe than those against masturbation, particularly by girls and married women.

5

"SELF-ABUSE"

If even the normal function of menstruation was surrounded in Victorian times with fear and self-consciousness, the sexual drive as manifest in masturbation was not only feared but dealt with harshly. The term "self-abuse" continued well into the twentieth century, even among sophisticated people.[1] It was believed that the practice in young children could lead to mental retardation and insanity. Precocious children were especially to be watched, for their imaginative little minds might lead them to all kinds of experiments! Catharine Beecher had as an informant Mrs. R. B. Gleason who had studied medicine and who managed a water-cure establishment in Elmira, New York. This severe woman advised that children be warned that "any fingering of the parts referred to involves terrible penalties."[2] It was a fearsome warning for a young person to carry into adult life.

In addition to such terrors as retardation and insanity, other effects of masturbation, such as indigestion, melancholy, and introspection, were listed. In extreme cases girls were required to wear chastity belts and boys a penal ring that would cause discomfort during an erection.

Dr. Bernard Talmey, who had a practice in New York City, gave detailed instruction for the prevention of masturbation. "No spicy foods, coffee, tea or cocoa—no bicycle riding. . . . Constipation and overloading of the bowels should be promptly relieved. . . . *No* erotic novels—no daydreaming."[3] Perhaps the endless needlework required of middle-class girls was also a form of insurance against "the solitary vice."

Dr. Talmey saw nothing wrong in invading an individual's privacy in order to check on possible masturbation; in fact he advocated close supervision. "The girl should never be allowed to remain in a bed when not asleep. She should not sleep on her back. She should not be allowed to remain any longer than necessary in the toilet or bathroom."[4] One can imagine the eye at the keyhole, the ear at the door, the voice reminding the sinner that much time has gone by in the bathroom.

Talmey, who was a gynecologist with the Metropolitan Hospital and Dispensary in New York, presented in his *Woman*, 1906, a case study of a "partially impotent woman whose frigidity and slight development of the clitoris were probably caused by the early practice of masturbation."[5]

He was one of the many Victorian physicians obsessed with the concept of the clitoris as a source of pleasure that competed with the more approved pleasure of sexual intercourse. In severe cases of masturbation, excision, cutting away, of part of the clitoris was performed.

It was theorized that women with a strong sexual drive would have an unusually large clitoris. However, several physicians studied the genital development of sexually active women and reported that the clitoris was not abnormally large in those individuals.[6]

Fundamentally, masturbation was bitterly opposed not only because it was believed to damage general health, particularly in children, but also because it was believed to diminish a wife's interest in, or acceptance of, intercourse with her husband. Mrs. Mary Gove Nichols, a practitioner of hydrotherapy, reported the case of a married woman who considered herself "pure . . . delivered from all temptation to a sensual life," and who wished that her husband would lose interest in sexual intercourse with her. Mrs. Nichols was indignant. "It is not natural or true," she declared, "for woman to be without the amative passion. . . . She is a diseased, and the disease had a cause."[7] The cause was either "atony of the nervous system from birth, or a diseased amativeness that causes solitary vice. . . . " In short, Mrs. Nichols believed that sexuality was normal in women, but that masturbation, "the solitary vice," was an improper and dangerous way to gratify it. She believed that sexual activity with a spouse was the only proper and normal sexual outlet.

Dr. Talmey, writing at the turn of the twentieth century, was even more brutal, "When a young woman shuns the company of males, it is well to bear in mind that she does so because she is an onanist or a sexual pervert."[8] The implication of perversion was so strong that many a masturbator submitted to incredibly harsh so-called cures. In a case study entitled "A remarkable cause of Nymphomania and its cure" (the problem is not nymphomania at all by today's standards, but rather obsession with masturbation), the sad account of a young married woman is given and quoted by Harvey Graham.[9]

The young woman is described as having had a miscarriage a few months after her wedding, followed by violent temper tantrums. The mother of the patient, enlisted by the doctor to watch her closely, discovered "with feelings none but the pureminded can appreciate" that her daughter masturbated. The patient "confessed" to the doctor, then became so open about masturbating that her mother tried "whipping her hands at the first movement for sexual gratification." Thus the mother acted like a policeman toward a grown daughter who had regressed to the forbidden pleasures of childhood. The transgression was viewed as all the more serious since the daughter preferred masturbation to sexual intercourse. Whether fear of another miscarriage colored the patient's sexual preference was explored not at all.

Many attempts were made to keep the patient from masturbating. The doctor used a carbolic acid solution that made her genitals sore, then "a pad . . . stuck full of sharp pins" so that the pain, if masturbation was attempted, would "bring her to her senses and aid to the moral suasion. . . ."

"Moral suasion?" Today we would regard as perverted such procedures as the infliction of pain to create behavioral change.

Electric shock was also tried, but the final resort was removal of the patient's ovaries, after permission in writing was received from the husband. Whether the patient gave *her* permission is not known, but after six months of seclusion she was reported by the doctor as "anxious to please" and to run her household. Either the brainwashing finally prevailed, or, relieved from the fear of pregnancy, if there had been such a fear, the patient then stabilized. What is clear and not speculative is that painful behavior modification measures and an ovariotomy were considered permissible in order to stop masturbation.

6

"THE AMATIVE IMPULSE"

A young lover in rural Pennsylvania described in his diary in 1861 the varied pleasures of lovemaking that he enjoyed on many nights until dawn, with the young woman of his affections.[1] So extensive were the activities that they may have included coitus interruptus, the most usual form of birth control. The young man clearly was yielding to "the amative impulse."

The view of the majority of Victorians was that "the amative impulse" ought to be indulged in only in moderation and only within marriage. Some wives enjoyed their sexuality; the middle-class wives surveyed by Dr. Clelia Mosher reported their satisfaction. They also said, all but three, that they practiced some form of birth control.[2] It is likely, therefore, that their sexual satisfaction was linked to lack of anxiety about pregnancy.

Occasionally there was advocacy of sexual foreplay, and books were available as early as the 1830's on physiology and methods of birth control. Charles Knowlton, a Massachusetts physician, as early as 1832 mentioned the condom but did not endorse it, since the materials available did not yet include vulcanized rubber.

The majority of authoritative Victorian writers on the subject of sexuality, both men and women, recommended restraint. Dr. Elizabeth Blackwell, who spoke with the authority of the first woman physician trained in the United States, noted "the astounding lust and cruelty of women uncontrolled by spiritual principle."[3] Alice B. Stockham, writing in the 1880's, warned that a wife should not be expected to act like a prostitute.[4]

Physicians, who viewed themselves as conservators of public morality, were united in their endorsement of moderation. Total abstinence, on the other hand, even after the birth of several children, was frowned upon, because it allegedly was responsible for heavy bleeding in women and engorgement of tissue in both men and women. Furthermore, "the male fluid" supposedly had a good effect on female organs. Intercourse was also said to prevent priapism in the male.

The tone of physicians, including Henry Putnam Stearns, superintendent of the prestigious mental hospital, the Hartford Retreat, founded in 1822 in Hartford, Connecticut, was prescriptive; they all declared marriage to be good medicine. The superintendent wrote that in his experience, persons who became "nervous, capricious, irritable, and hysterical," were generally from "the unmarried class." He continued in *Insanity: Its Cause and Prevention*: "The condition of marriage is doubtless the normal one for both sexes, and, as a rule, a larger degree of physical health is enjoyed by persons who live in this relation."[5]

Physicians condemned "animal manifestations." They warned against love becoming "carnalized" and recommended instead the "enhancement of love's Platonic form."[6] Clearly they were uneasy about pleasure in sexual intercourse. They warned furthermore that if "the female is amatively excited . . . the ripening of the ova may be hastened."[7] Therefore, the woman who enjoyed sexual intercourse was burdened with the fear of "hastened" ripening of ova and hence an unexpected pregnancy. Declared the doctors, "The use of marriage or the sexual act for mere pleasure, and using any means to avoid impregnation, are unnatural."[8]

Furthermore, the severe doctors continued, "It is not necessary that there should be any enjoyment of coition on the part of the female. . . . It may take place in sleep, or other insensibility."[9] In short, the sexual act was implied to be so unattractive to a proper woman that she might prefer to be, or to act, unconscious during the event. It is no wonder that Catharine Beecher's friends wept when their innocent daughters entered matrimony. It would seem that aggressive lovers, like Mabel Loomis Todd in Andover, Massachusetts, were the exception rather than the rule, and that their spouses were more inventive, certainly more compliant, than the average.

Just as temperance in alcohol consumption grew as a movement during the nineteenth century, so did advocacy of moderation in sexual intercourse. What Carl Degler describes loosely as "The Social Purity Movement" advanced markedly. One by-product was more consideration of the wife: a husband, declared Ida B. Craddock, ought to be trained "to wait for" his wife.[10] When, in 1895, a group of doctors stated that continence was not harmful to men, the medical establishment gave in effect its approval of a single standard of sexual restraint.[11] Yet some doctors continued to state that abstaining "is easily done by most women and many men," implying a feeble sexual drive in women.[12]

Liberated women, like Elizabeth Cady Stanton, were angry at this attitude. She criticized even Walt Whitman, whose *Leaves of Grass* with its celebration of sexuality had shocked literate America, because he was "ignorant of the great natural fact that a healthy woman has as much passion as a man, that she needs nothing stronger than the law of attraction to draw her to the male."[13]

Stanton rejected the Victorian idea that a woman's role was merely to submit to a man's desire. She said boldly, "The fact is the seduction is, and ought to be, mutual. No love is without seduction in its highest sense." So much, Stanton implied, for the belief that woman is "insensible" to sexuality!

As late as her sixty-sixth year, she wrote in her diary: "I have come to the conclusion that the first great work to be accomplished for woman is to revolutionize the dogma that sex is a crime, marriage a defilement and maternity a bane."[14] Stanton, probably most successfully of any American woman of the time, combined acceptance of natural drives with social reforms based on reason and equity. The radical feminist, Victoria Woodhull, went even further, declaring in *Woodhull and Claflin's Weekly*, November 2, 1872, that "the amative impulse is the physiological basis of character."

In a climate of black and white choices, with little gray, prostitution flourished. A curious way of measuring its incidence was a per capita figure: in mid-century, the incidence in the United States was estimated as one in fifty-two.[15] From time to time, committees on "social purity" were set up, and some committees advocated the licensing of brothels, European-style. But St. Louis, from 1870 to 1873, was the only American city to adopt the measure.

Brothels abounded in large cities. In New York, a street notorious for them was Greene Street. More elegant brothels, called "parlor houses," were found uptown. One of the madams, proud of running "a first class house," wrote a letter in 1871 to Victoria Woodhull, who was then editor of *Woodhull and Claflin's Weekly*, after listening to Woodhull's fiery lecture in Steinway Hall in New York on "The Principles of Social Freedom." The madam, who identified herself as Mary Bowles, had kept the house, she said, "eleven or twelve years." Her clients ranged "from doctors of divinity to counterjumpers." What the clients did not know was that Ms. Bowles kept two ledgers which listed all their names and addresses. For her own amusement, she even employed a detective to follow clients to their homes and offices.[16]

Probably the most infamous brownstone in New York City was the one on Fifth Avenue and Fifty-second Street, which belonged to the most famous local abortionist, Madame Restell. Anthony Comstock, a self-appointed crusader against contraceptive devices and abortionists, arrested Madame Restell. She tried to bribe him, failed, and foreseeing ruin, chose suicide. After her death, a sardonic cartoon appeared, captioned "Fifth Avenue a year after the death of Madame Restell." It shows a Fifth Avenue jammed with pregnant women and babies in carriages![17]

Less blunt than brothels, simply places where strangers could meet and arrange appointments, were the "concert saloons." Drinking and dancing and entertainment were available. The waitresses were pretty women whose usual costume, no matter which saloon they worked for, consisted of a short skirt, a low-necked blouse, and high red boots with tassels.

Clearly sexual attitudes were modified by social and economic class, as Dr. Elizabeth Blackwell so coolly remarked, and one physician who was studying the causes of prostitution insisted that economics rather than "inclination" led the prostitute into her occupation.[18] It was the poor girl who was tempted most often by prostitution, just as it was the middle-class girl, carefully watched and chaperoned, who bought and read the books that warned her against sexual indulgence and that implied, or even said flatly, that "the amative impulse" was something to be wary of.

"The amative impulse" was treated gingerly in fiction, although not in pornography.[19] Indeed, much fiction about young well-born women portrays them on the verge of shock when in the embrace of a male, even of a fiancé. When Newland Archer in Edith Wharton's *Age of Innocence* kisses his fiancé on the lips for the first time, she is "disturbed."

> To Archer's strained nerves the vision of May Welland was as soothing as the sight of the blue sky and the lazy river. They sat down on a bench under the orange-trees and he put his arm about her and kissed her. It was like drinking at a cold spring with the sun on it; but his pressure may have been more vehement than he had intended, for the blood rose to her face and she drew back as if he had startled her . . . he saw that she was disturbed, and shaken out of her cool boyish composure.[20]

Archer has mixed feelings about May. On the one hand, he is stimulated at the prospect of initiating a virgin into the realities of sexuality. When they are first engaged, he looks at her as she blushes during a romantic scene in an opera. "He contemplated her absorbed young face with a thrill of possessorship in which pride in his own masculine initiation was mingled with a tender reverence for her abysmal purity."

"Possessorship"—Ownership—The sexually untouched female owned by a sexually experienced male. Newland is no philanderer; however, he has had the discreet affairs standard for his set. He knows that when he is ready to choose the mother of the children who will inherit his name and his property, he will choose a well-bred innocent. Such a person is May. She is submissive to mother and father and even postpones her wedding date so that all her monogrammed linens (dozens and dozens of sheets, pillowcases and napkins) will be ready. Scarcely a passionate bride.

Newland Archer feels "tender reverence," but he also feels imprisoned by the conventions of his engagement: " . . . he felt himself oppressed by this creation of factitious purity, so cunningly manufactured by a conspiracy of mothers and aunts and grandmothers and long-dead ancestresses, because it was supposed to be what he wanted. . . . " He regrets that because of the conventions of his class, he and his fiancé know very little about each other. "What could he and she really know of each other, since it was his duty, as a 'decent' fellow, to conceal his past from her, and hers, as a marriageable girl, to have no past to conceal?" He fears for the future of their marriage: it will be like all the others he knows, "a dull association of material and social interests held together by ignorance on the one side and hypocrisy on the other."

After his marriage, he becomes increasingly troubled by the voluptuousness and easy manners of a liberated woman, Countess Olenska. On the brink of an extramarital affair with the Countess, he remains faithful to his wife when he learns that she is pregnant. Yet he is tortured by fantasies and a sense of the loss of freedom. He has a fantasy of his wife dying: "If she were going to die—to die soon—and leave him free!" The book ends with him in his later years, a pillar of society.

Occasionally women writers dared to suggest that women enjoyed sexual feelings even with a stranger. Kate O'Flaherty Chopin, in the short story, "A Shameful Affair," describes a proper young woman, Mildred, lounging her way through a hot Southern summer. Mildred thinks of herself as emancipated: she has read Ibsen and Browning. But she has always kept her behavior with men under tight control, until one day she notices a farmhand "young and brown . . . with nice blue eyes." Normally she ignores men of a lower social class than her own: "Farmhands are not so very nice to look at, and she was nothing of an anthropologist."

But on an unforgettable day she takes a long walk and comes upon the young man as he is fishing. She asks to hold the pole. (A psychoanalytic interpretation here is hazardous!) As the young farmhand instructs Mildred in the craft of fishing, their hands touch and he looks for an instant into "a pair of young, dark eyes that gleamed for an instant unconscious things into his own." The young people embrace. Mildred feels afterwards that her "chaste lips" have been "rifled" of their innocence. Yet there has been the "unconscious" signal of readiness. She now has a "hateful burden to bear alone." It is also a "sweet trouble."

Part of her problem is that the young man is not a suitable lover. But Chopin chooses not to pursue this aspect and indeed changes it by disclosing that the young worker is really a talented student who has chosen to do rough outdoor work for the summer.

This information, which Mildred receives by letter, serves to move the young man into an "acceptable" social class, but still Mildred cannot deal with the memory of the kiss. The carnal offends her, even though the young man is now socially acceptable. She thinks of him as the "offender," and the word is placed in capital letters.

The young man finally does the conventional thing; he apologizes to her for yielding to the impulse to kiss her, and he asks her to forgive and forget: " . . . since you are willing to forget, you will be generous enough to forgive the offender some day?"

This is the conventional apology of the time from a young man who has taken a liberty, but it is followed by an unconventional reply from Mildred: "Some day . . . perhaps, when I shall have forgiven myself." With this relatively daring reply, Mildred acknowledges that she has not been a *victim* of the man's ardor, but that she had wanted his embrace. She has been a participant, not a victim, in a situation in which the proper Victorian girl was supposed to have feelings of outrage and indignation.

As both Elizabeth Stanton and Victoria Woodhull noted, "the amative impulse" could be repressed in some Victorian women, but it could not always be obliterated. It is ironic that fashion accentuated the curves and fullnesses of the female body in an era when for the middle class at least, the message was to think of higher things. Dr. Bernard Talmey of New York City, although often insensitive about the feelings of women, was able, on the subject of fashion at least, to say some very sensible words. Of the corset, he remarked, it "aims to render conspicuous and prominent the specific female organ, the bosom." Talmey continued, "The combination of the bustle with the stretching of the skirt over the abdomen . . . was surely invented by a Parisian demi-monde to serve sensuality."[21]

Woman's fashion invited what woman's upbringing rejected. Yet even for the woman who enjoyed her sexuality, sexual intercourse was often accompanied by fear—fear of pregnancy and fear of childbirth. Furthermore, the physicians and other authority figures who told her that both strong sexual drive and weak sexual drive were unhealthy added that avoidance of pregnancy in marriage was immoral and dangerous.

7

"IN THE FAMILY WAY"

It was because of the death of a baby boy during his mother's labor of fifty-two hours that Victoria became Queen of England. Young Princess Charlotte and her infant both died as a result of the agonizing labor and birth.

Charlotte was the only daughter of George IV of England, and when she married Leopold, later king of the Belgians, she hoped for a male heir. She was twenty when she married, and a year and a half later, she delivered a dead baby. She died soon afterwards.

A distinguished British obstetrician had attended her, Sir Richard Croft. Like so many physicians who feared to use forceps—so many mutilated babies and mothers had they seen after forceps delivery—he did not intervene early enough with instruments. Three months later, in deep melancholy, he committed suicide. Thus, the royal succession passed in 1819 to the infant princess Victoria, who would reign from 1837 to 1901.

Infant mortality today in the United States is approximately sixteen per thousand live births, or one and a half percent. A hundred years ago ten times as many infants died. In Colonial times, the infant death rate was fifty per cent, no better than tossing a coin. And although families were large in those days, there is no rule that the number of survivors defines the degree of grief. In the diary of Elizabeth Drinker, a Quaker who kept a diary between 1758 and 1807, telling largely of the medical events in the lives of her nine children and twenty-five grandchildren, she writes sadly after the death of her daughter Sally: " . . . my beloved Sally is in her grave . . . in the 46th year of her age. . . . Oh! what a loss to a mother near 72 years of age, my first born darling—my first, my 3rd, my 5th, 7th, and 9th are in their graves. My 2'd, 4th, 6th and 8th are living."[1]

Most married women in Colonial times were pregnant or nursing for all their years until menopause. Some nursed because they believed that a nursing mother would not become pregnant. Others nursed their children, or paid a wet nurse to do it, because a child was more likely to survive with breast milk than cow's milk, which was frequently contaminated. Furthermore, as a simple practical matter, cow's milk was undependable because it went sour in a few hours on a hot summer's day.

Elizabeth Drinker, who mourned her Sally, had her last child when she was forty-nine, in 1784. Thereafter, she was an invalid and had to remain at home. She may have developed the dreaded vesico-vaginal fistula, the breakdown of tissue after difficult labors and poor midwifery that caused urine to ooze out of the bladder and dribble from the vagina, so that the affected woman became virtually a social outcast, odiferous, forced to wear a kind of diaper, and eternally suffering from the equivalent of diaper rash. When in 1852 Dr. James Marion Sims, a surgeon in Alabama, published his paper on repairing vesico-vaginal fistula, after four years of experimenting and operating, it signaled the coming out of the dark and smelly closet of the women through the generations who had suffered from incontinence.

What Sims found was extraordinary, and the publication of his paper in the distinguished *American Journal of Medical Science* caused other physicians to adopt his procedures. The first phase was the discovery that the knee-chest position for vaginal examination created a suction in the pelvis that caused air to dilate the vagina to its maximum. Thus the physician with the aid, first of a pewter spoon, later with a more sophisticated instrument, could really observe a fistula. (Yet, ironically, conservative gynecologists, such as Charles Meigs, thought that a proper lady ought to object to a pelvic examination because of her tender sensibility.)

Sims was elated with his discoveries, foreseeing the relief of "the loveliest of all God's creatures of one of the most loathesome maladies that can possibly befall poor human nature." For four years, Sims experimented with kinds of sutures and the means to hold the knots in the tissue while healing proceeded.

Silk thread did not hold. Silver wire did. Recollection of the ordinary metal shot or sinker he had used in fishing for holding the line gave Sims the solution for the problem of holding knots fast in the tissue.

> I had been lying awake for an hour, wondering how to tie the suture, when all at once an idea occured to me to run shot, a perforated shot, on the suture, and, when it was drawn tight to compress it with a pair of forceps, which would make the knot perfectly secure.[2]

After publication of his article, which was widely read, Sims moved to New York City and, in 1855, established the Women's Hospital, which drew women patients from all over the United States. More than half of the women treated for vesico-vaginal fistula in the first few years of the hospital's existence were immigrants, poor women who had been arriving from Europe by the hundreds of thousands from the 1840's onward.

Untreated vesico-vaginal fistula had made life a misery for women until Sims' procedures were widely used. Puerperal fever, "Childbed fever," however, was the killer.

Early in the nineteenth century perceptive physicians had observed that doctors and nurses who went from the bedside or autopsy chamber of a mother with puerperal fever to well patients who had just delivered babies soon reported cases of the fever among the formerly well patients. This observation led Dr. Oliver Wendell Holmes and others to suppose a "contagion" and to suggest that careful washing of hands and changing of clothes after being with a sick or dead patient would prevent the contagion spreading to other mothers. After all, Dr. Holmes reasoned, the separation of the placenta, the afterbirth, from the uterus leaves a kind of wound, vulnerable to infection. Dr. Holmes, who was a man of letters as well as a physician, came to his conclusions by dint of detective work, but he was laughed at by many physicians. After all, they said, a doctor was a gentlemen and didn't need to be reminded to work with clean hands![3]

Unfortunately, Dr. Holmes' article was not widely noticed, because it was first published in a small journal. But in 1855 he reissued and enlarged the article. Although he and those who agreed with him were mocked and called "The Contagionists," recognition was on the way. In France, Louis Pasteur had been working on minute organisms in a study of putrefaction, and in Glasgow Infirmary, Joseph Lister noted sadly that within a day of a successful operation, a patient was often dead from infection—from gangrene, blood poisoning, or "erysipelas," a name then given to any inflammation of tissue. Lister observed that patients *within* a hospital were much more likely to develop infection of their wounds than were private patients *outside* the hospital. He studied Pasteur's work and decided that something in the air contaminated wounds. He noted that a compound fracture (when the bone protrudes through the skin) was usually followed by infection, whereas a simple fracture (when the bone is protected by skin) was usually infection-free.

Organisms could be destroyed by great heat or by chemicals. Great heat was obviously ruled out. Lister used instead a solution of carbolic acid for washing skin and instruments. His first major paper on antisepsis appeared in 1867 in the British journal *Lancet*; this marked the beginning of the conquest of infection, including that terrible killer of mothers, puerperal fever. By 1884, an obstetrician in Dublin who used antisepsis and who kept careful records on over a thousand deliveries reported a maternal death rate of only half of one per cent.

The concept of microorganisms that caused disease and infection was a tremendous step forward. For centuries, even well into the nineteenth century, when outbreaks of cholera or yellow fever raged through cities, those who could, simply fled; those who couldn't burned fires that supposedly would stop the contagion. For example, in 1849, when Harriet Beecher Stowe was living in Cincinnati and cholera killed over a thousand people in the city in one day, she observed fires stoked with soft coal burning on street corners in the hope that the "miasma" created would stop the "contagion." In larger cities, where masses of people congregated and laissez-faire government was lenient, epidemics of cholera, typhus, and typhoid continued late into the century. Only gradually were public health measures set up and enforced.

One of the great scientific discoveries led to the prevention of blindness in babies delivered by mothers with gonorrhea. In 1879, Albert Neisser identified the genococcus, an organism that lives in mucous membranes. An infant born of a woman with venereal disease develops the infection during birth, as the child passes through the infected birth canal. The infection lodges in the lining of the eye and produces scarring and blindness. Five years after Neisser's discovery, Carl Crede of Leipzig described a method of preventing such blindness; a single drop in each eye of the newborn of a two per cent solution of silver nitrate. Very simple, seemingly. But for centuries before, infants delivered of infected mothers had become blind for life.

Isolating microorganisms that carried disease was a great advance, for then antitoxins could be sought. The killer of infants, diptheria, often known as "putrid sore throat," was isolated as a bacillus in 1884, and six years later an antitoxin was developed.

Tuberculosis, or pulmonary consumption, as it was usually called, took longer, indeed until the twentieth century, to conquer. In Colonial and early Victorian times not only was the tuberculosis patient not isolated, but remained in very close contact with servants and members of the family. A good mother (not father) or a dutiful servant often slept in the same room during the most severe blood-spitting episodes of the patient and even shared his bed. William Drinker, one of Elizabeth Drinker's sons, had a long siege of tuberculosis and remained in close contact with his family. Curiously, horsebackriding and other exercise rather than rest were then regarded as helpful.[4]

The usual treatment of tuberculosis for most of the century was the old treatment for most illnesses: purges, herb-taking, and bloodletting by leech or by vein. Dr. Benjamin Rush, a distinguished Philadelphia physician, believed in massive bloodletting, especially to treat puerperal fever and profuse menstruation. From one patient, he drew a half pint of blood fifteen times in six weeks! He also prescribed castor oil in large doses or 180 grains of calomel, or ninety grains of quinine for purging patients. For bloodletting, dozens of leeches were used.[5] A sick person had to be very strong indeed to survive such treatments!

Heroic endurance of pain, or else fainting, were the alternatives for a patient in surgery until the discovery of nitrous oxide (sometimes called laughing gas), ether, and chloroform. Previously laudanum, an opium derivative, had been used, but the dosage of laudanum could not be readily controlled. The use of nitrous oxide began as a public spectacle, for an admission fee, an exhibition of the silly behavior of people who had sniffed the gas. But Dr. Horace Wells, a dentist from Hartford, Connecticut, and later William Morton of Boston experimented with inhaled sulphuric ether. Ethics became involved; Morton wanted to patent his product, which he named "Letheon." (This was a poetic but inappropriate name, since this special sleep led to life, not death.) Litigation dragged on but finally anesthesia was used around the world, not only preventing pain, but preventing the deaths that came from the patients' going into shock.

Improvements came in gynecology and obstetrics as the nineteenth century wore on. Successful operations for Caesarean section and ovariotomy were recorded. Birth by section had been known in antiquity, but for generations the living infant was usually taken from a dead mother.

Another horror for the childbearing veteran was the prolapsed uterus, a uterus that descended and sometimes hung like a scrotum, usually after long and difficult labors. By the end of the nineteenth century, repairs could be safely made, because of the development of anesthesia and antisepsis. For centuries pessaries had been used, from small plugs to half a pomegranate, to shove the uterus upwards. Women had even been tied to ladders and hung upside down, so that the uterus would return to its high position! But all these methods gave at best only temporary relief and were often traumatic. Until the end of the nineteenth century, a damaged reproductive system turned many a woman into a permanent invalid.

It should be remembered that even after the great advances in obstetrics and gynecology by the 1870's, the large hospitals were the places likely to have staff informed about the new techniques and able to use them. Less equipped were general practitioners scattered throughout the country. It was not necessarily a question of who could afford to pay for certain procedures; a poor immigrant woman treated at Women's Hospital in New York City after 1855 probably received more advanced treatment than a middle-class woman in a small town.

As treatment for the diseases of women progressed, the demand for contraception also increased, much to the anger of conservatives, both medical and lay people.

For centuries a series of beliefs about fertility had been accumulating, which were revealed later, as microbiology developed, to be quite incorrect. A major belief was that a nursing mother would not become pregnant. This was a very old belief, and it explains the advice the Elizabeth Drinker gave to a melancholy daughter who was about to begin labor. "I endeavor'd to talk her into better spirits, told her that . . . she was now in her 39th year, & that this might possibly be the last trial of this sort, if she could suckle her baby for 2 years to come as she had several times done heretofore. . . . "[6]

Another belief that persisted late into the nineteenth century was that fertility in women was as it is with other mammals, with the fertile days close to menstruation. Theoretically, then, mid-cycle would be a "safe" time for intercourse. Later, observation of ovulation in women showed the reverse to be true. Many a Victorian woman was astounded to find herself pregnant after having intercourse during the supposedly "safe" period.

The problem for fertile women was not only the number of children but the spacing. As clever a woman as Harriet Beecher Stowe had twins nine months after she was married, then another child the following year, a fourth child two years later, and a fifth three years later, in 1843. From that time until 1848, when her sixth child was born, she was intermittently melancholy and spent almost a year at the Brattleboro Hydropathic Institute in Vermont. Within a short time of her return to her family in Cincinnati, she was again pregnant.

Her sister, Catharine, who never married, implied that Harriet was overwhelmed with child care. This was so even though Harriet had a maid helping at home, and one of the twins lived away from home in the care of a wet nurse. Clearly not only poor women, but middle-class women as well, were quite exhausted if they had a large family of children close in age.

Catharine wrote to her sister, Mary Beecher Perkins, in 1837, describing Harriet's situation in Cincinnati, married to poor Professor Calvin Stowe, whose salary then averaged about five hundred dollars a year, although he knew more about the Old Testament, and about classical languages, than most scholars in the United States.

> Harriet has one baby put out for the winter, the other at home, and number three will be here the middle of January. Poor thing, she bears up wonderfully well, and I hope will live through this first tug of matrimonial warfare, and then she says she shall not have any more children, she knows for certain, for one while. Though how she found this out I cannot say, but she seems quite confident about it.[7]

"Poor thing" obviously was unsuccessful in avoiding pregnancy, for in spite of her being "confident," she was pregnant again within a year.

Conservative physicians, like the authors of *The Glory of Woman*, were still writing as late as 1896 that the only dependable and safe way of avoiding pregnancy was abstinence and their brief description of the alleged "safe" period included, because of the limitations of the microscope, days of the fertile period. Meanwhile a best-selling physician-writer, Dr. William Goodell, thundered, "There are no harmless ways in which gestation can be interrupted or conception shunned."[8]

Behind the anger of physicians who condemned birth control was often the fear that immigrants would control the nation because of their many children. The anger and fear are manifest in a lecture given by Dr. Goodell before the Medical and Chirurgical Faculty of Maryland, reprinted in book form in 1882 as *The Dangers and Duty of the Hour*. He was also a professor of Clinical and Didactic Gynecology at the University of Pennsylvania.

Goodell said angrily that the native-born Yankee population was practicing "the indecencies of married life," and declared, "Unless by some means a change is wrought in this particular, the Irish, the Germans, and their descendants will occupy the land." He was appalled by the shrinking birthrate of Yankees and native-born families. He stated that in a study of several generations in Lowell, Massachusetts, the once-great mill town, the first generation averaged eight to ten children, the next three generations, seven children, and the fifth generation, "less than three." Clearly the Yankee women of his day were practicing birth control. Goodell declared, "The family idea is drifting into individualism," and he called "the avoidance of offspring" no less than "a damnable sin."[9]

He was also shocked at the divorce rate in New England, one divorce to twelve marriages. In Massachusetts, he said, the divorce rate had doubled; in Vermont and Connecticut, it had increased by a third. Furthermore, he said, many of the native-born women who had children were unable or unwilling to suckle them and "should the child survive, it is suckled by aliens."[10]

Immigrants were feared and looked down upon by Goodell and many others. Between 1846 and 1860, almost four million immigrants entered the United States, and in 1860 the population was over thirty-one million, having jumped from twenty-three million ten years before. This was the largest increase in any single decade in United States history.

Cities were bursting with immigrant poor. Able-bodied men could always find heavy work, laying tracks for railroads, digging canals, hewing and laying cobblestones. But the sick, and many women and children, became casualties, along with the disabled veterans of the Civil War. They lived in such crowded tenements as the radical feminist, Victoria Woodhull, described, "a six-story tenement house, one hundred feet front by seventy deep, which contains five hundred men, women, and children having no regular employment. . . . "[11] In Hartford, the capital of Connecticut, there was in the 1870's one short street where 721 people lived. Three hundred twenty of the residents of the street were under the age of sixteen! Of the thirty-seven thousand people in that city, one-third were foreign-born.

Physicians like Edward B. Foote, who studied the birth and death rate in New York City in the 1880's, were appalled by the increasing numbers of "sickly, deformed, and idiotic children that become wards of the state." He continued, "Instead of thirty children born with a net result at the end of twenty years of twelve living ones, it would be better that there should be only fifteen born, and these so well cared for that twelve would survive."[12] According to his figures, then, the death rate for poor youth under age twenty in the cities was forty to fifty per cent!

The conditions of the poor were pitiable, with swarming families and ever-present death and disease, which Catharine Beecher, Jacob Riis, Victoria Woodhull, and others described with horror. Amateur abortion produced a death rate fifteen per cent higher than the maternal death rate.[13] Meanwhile, middle-class doctors damned the middle- and upper-class women who practiced contraception, and Anthony Comstock railed against both abortion and contraception.

Even in sermons, fear of an increasing criminal class among the poor was proclaimed, while at the same time the middle-class birth rate was shrinking. A minister preaching to a congregation in Connecticut in 1876 quoted statistics from the *New York Times* on the criminality in descendants of one woman, "who died about fifty years ago." "There exists among us a criminal class—a body of people who are the enemies of society. It is hereditary. Boys and girls are born into it, just as any other class of society. They are educated in it—they receive the training, moral and mental, which their class sees fit to give them."[14] The minister did not believe that the "criminal class" was confined to immigrants; in fact he mentioned a family of five generations in the United States who over those years had produced "76 convicted criminals, 180 disreputable persons, and 206 paupers."

Clearly he was fearful about what would happen and was happening to American society, yet he concluded on a positive note, "Society cannot afford to be hopeless, and Christian society dare not and cannot be cruel." Although there was fear that the uneducated and fertile immigrant poor would dominate the nation, there was also before the Civil War a determination by many slave owners that female slaves should breed prolifically, to increase the master's riches.[15]

Among the popular "artifices" used—Dr. Goodell called them "the equipment of the brothel"[16]—there was by mid-century the condom made of rubber, although in earlier generations it had been made from silk or pig's bladder. The most practiced method of birth control, however, was coitus interruptus, intercourse with ejaculation taking place outside the vagina. This method demanded of both partners great self-control, and according to one medical writer, "the woman eventually became a nervous wreck."[17] She could never be sure, of course, whether ejaculation could be postponed, so that contraceptive technique took precedence over enjoyment. The Karezza method, popularized by John Humphrey Noyes, permitted sexual stroking to go on for hours, with resting as needed, and always short of ejaculation. The method was of interest to some Victorians, but it was scarcely a major method of birth control.

The only birth control methods that a woman herself could control were the douche and the vaginal sponge. Until 1873 and the Comstock law, which was entitled, "An Act for the Suppression of Trade in, and Circulation of Obscene Literature and Articles of Immoral Use," newspapers and magazines regularly published advertisements for douche materials, vaginal suppositories, and abortifacients. But many methods and products were useless, and some chemicals used were dangerous. Despite these limitations there were so many readers of medical manuals that included advice on birth control that these books became best-sellers. Edward B. Foote's *Medical Common Sense*, first published in 1858, was widely read, and by the end of the century a quarter of a million copies had been sold. Similar books by Robert Dale Owen and Charles Knowlton were known even earlier. Birth control was clearly a subject of major interest for Victorians, although many of the methods were either unsafe or ineffective, or both.

When a woman decided to abort a pregnancy, there were as always abortionists available. It was estimated that in Victorian America the death rate from abortion, self-induced or done by others, was fifteen times the maternal death rate. Abortions could be had for as little as ten dollars, or for much more in such elegant establishments as Madame Restell's town house on Fifth Avenue in New York City. Her fees were so high that she was able to leave an estate of a million dollars. There are no dependable statistics about abortion in American Victorian times, but the increasing number of stillbirths recorded for New York City—in 1868, 105 per one thousand deaths, as compared with 25 per one thousand in 1808–09—makes it a reasonable assumption that abortions, self-induced or performed by others, increased in the population as the century moved on.[18]

A usual method to induce abortion was one similar to that used today, to inject the uterus with water. The injection was followed by heavy bleeding. An exotic method, advertised by druggists, was an electrocution kit. The method was to place one pole on the abdomen and the other in a glass rod in the cervix.[19] There is no way of knowing how popular or effective this bizarre method was.

Folk methods for abortion had been used for generations—the eating of mallow, motherwort, tansy and other plants, which caused severe intestinal cramping and diarrhea, and eventually miscarriage. Cantharides (Spanish flies) had been known for centuries. Although lethal in large quantity, it was still used as an abortifacient. The horrible knitting needle, and sharp wire, were used then, as they still are, as instruments of last resort. Manic dancing, self-induced falls, horsebackriding, and even punching and high jumps, were also used, as they had been for centuries, to induce abortion.

There were state laws such as the one passed in Pennsylvania in 1860 that made abortion punishable by fine and solitary confinement for from three to five years, but such statutes were not regularly enforced: there were too many methods to control, and little proof. The American Medical Association, however, in 1871 bitterly criticized women who sought abortions as undutiful and murderous.[20]

Anxious over the possibility of frequent pregnancies, criticized by authoritative males if birth control was practiced, for these and for a variety of reasons, a large number of women became depressed—"melancholy"—and for relief paid visits to male medical practitioners or fled their families and went to "water cure" and other establishments.

The water-bath "cures" were based upon baths, hot- and cold-water packs, and, above all, the comradeship of women with similar problems. Harriet Beecher Stowe remained in a water-bath sanatorium in Brattleboro, Vermont for almost one year, in 1846. Her half-sister, Isabella Beecher Hooker, first went to a water-cure establishment in 1853, in Florence, Massachusetts. Later, in 1860, she visited the well-known establishment of Mrs. R. B. Gleason, in Elmira, New York. Among the women who took this cure were also Mrs. Dickinson, mother of Emily, and Olivia Langdon Clemens, wife of Mark Twain. A stay at a water-bath facility clearly was an accepted event for a middle-class woman.

8

THE WORLD AS SICKROOM

It is clear that Victorian women had a good deal to be fearful about, particularly if they had numerous pregnancies. The maternal death rate, informally presented by a practicing obstetrician in the nineties, was given as "thousands after having borne two or three children."[1] True, the life expectancy of women was higher by two years than men's—forty-three years as against forty-one—but the high maternal death rate and abortion rate estimated as fifteen times higher[2] was compensated for statistically by the large number of single women who generally lived longer than the married.

The dangers of motherhood, much publicized in medical books for lay readers, were many, but there is no reason to think that Victorian women were any feebler than their forebears; their illnesses simply received more publicity in an age of cheap printing. For example, as early as 1843, harrowing case histories of women with female diseases were published in Dr. Samuel Ashwell's *Diseases Peculiar to Woman*, part of the Massachusetts Medical Society's Library of Practical Medicine. This was a book intended for physicians. Case 30 is the history of a washerwoman suffering from chronic heavy bleeding, with many children and frequent pregnancies. She is typical of the woman of many pregnancies who barely managed to stay alive. None of the remedies of her physician was of much use. In despair the patient refused the last resort, "tow," the short fibers of hemp or flax, used to plug the vagina to prevent further heavy bleeding. Like most physicians, Dr. Ashwell believed that abstinence from intercourse as well as interrupted intercourse contributed to female diseases. "Abstinence produces congestion of ovaria and uterus," he declared.[3]

Later in the nineteenth century many thoughtful women who were mothers of grown daughters wondered why the new generation was apprehensive about motherhood, so mindful of death and dying. Self-made women, like Harriet Beecher Stowe, looked back upon their own past and the hard apprenticeship of running a house and raising children, and puzzled over the seeming fragility of their daughters.

In "The Lady Who Does Her Own Work," printed in *The Atlantic Monthly* in 1864, Mrs. Stowe puts into the mouth of a young narrator named Marianne some pious yearnings.

> I wish I had been brought up so . . . and had all the strength and adroitness that those women had. I should not dread to begin housekeeping, as I now do. I should feel myself independent. I should feel that I knew how to direct my servants, and what it was reasonable and proper to expect of them.[4]

In writing the article, Harriet ignored or repressed the fact that her own mother had been loving but tubercular, fragile, and carried off early to her grave, and that her father-in-law had been four times a widower. Harriet also ignored, or repressed, the memory of her own sick headaches, her temporary blindness, her melancholy letters, and the year at a watercure establishment, during her long stage of childbearing and childraising. Like so many people successful at last, she rationalized her earlier melancholy, and endowed the past, her own and that of her forebears, with a heroic and rosy cast that in reality it never possessed.

Important and successful, in 1870 she became worried at the "confirmed melancholy" into which her daughter, Georgiana, seemed ready to slip after the birth of her first child. To her sister, Mary Perkins, she confided that Georgie had become "perfectly morbid," even though her "womb" was in "a remarkably strong healthy state." Harriet went on, "I think nothing is the matter with her" and said that air and exercise would help![5] Again, she forgot the morbidity of her own earlier thoughts.

That she had suffered deeply from the illness and death of her infant son, Charley, is clear from her letters. After the child's death, she wrote that he was the only child she had been able to nurse from both breasts; nor did the birth of another son a year later, to whom she gave almost the same name, erase her terrible sense of loss. She wrote to a friend in 1850, "I often think what you said to me—that another child would not fill the place of the old—that it would be another interest & another love—so I find it."[6]

Like many Victorian women, and others before and since, when the death of a child had to be dealt with, Harriet had been without her husband, alone in frightening circumstances. When a cholera epidemic struck again in 1849—it had swept through Cincinnati and the South, especially in cities, year after year—Harriet tended the sick in her household: first the laundress, then one-year-old Charley. He sweated; then he shivered. Harriet sat at his side when she wasn't giving him sponge baths and changing his sheets. Black clouds of smoke drifted over the rooftops from the soft coal that people burned at street corners in the hope that the smoke would destroy the "miasma," whatever that was. Hearses rumbled through the city.

When Charley died, Harriet sewed his shroud as she also had sewed the shroud for the laundress. Although in her writing she was capable of beautifying dying, she was also capable of some stark perceptions. One of the strongest passages in *Uncle Tom's Cabin* is the aftermath of the death of old Prue, who, tipsy and confused, fell down the cellar stairs. "The flies got to her," wrote Harriet bluntly. Yet Eva's death she treated sentimentally.

Harriet wanted to accept her son's death as God's will. To her husband, she wrote, "I write as though there were no sorrow like my sorrow. . . ."[7] She remembered in 1853, four years after her son's death, and after the publication of the book that made her famous, the agony she had been through in Cincinnati. To Mrs. Eliza Follen of Boston she wrote,

" . . . much that is in that book [*Uncle Tom's Cabin*] had its root in the awful scenes and bitter sorrows of that summer."[8]

It may be difficult for the modern reader to find moving the passages in *Uncle Tom's Cabin* in which Mrs. Bird rummages among the baby clothes of her dead child for garments for Eliza's child. But a Victorian mother, no matter what her social class, was likely to have experienced the loss of a child; and such a mother is addressed by the author: "And oh, mother that reads this, has there never been in your house a drawer, or a closet, the opening again of which has been to you like the opening again of a little grave?"

Extended passages on the deaths of children are found in many Victorian letters and diaries. An entire chapter is devoted to the loss of children in Lydia H. Sigourney's book *Letters to Mothers*, which was already in it sixth edition in 1854. "If they [the children] died in the Redeemer, and you live in obedience to his commands, how rapturous will be the everlasting embrace in which you shall enfold them."[9] Religion gave comfort to many people, but as Harriet Beecher Stowe's long mourning suggests, the consolation of religion did not always erase the sense of loss.

For Harriet Stowe, Elizabeth Stanton, and other ambitious women, having children was fulfilling, but the many child-bearing years also drained them of energy that they knew they could have used differently. Harriet believed long before 1852 and her sudden success with *Uncle Tom's Cabin* that she had writing ability. Although not well known, she had been published; she was, therefore, justified in taking herself seriously as a writer. Yet the work and responsibility for her large family sometimes was too much for her. Several years after her long rest cure, in 1851 she wrote from Brunswick, Maine, to her husband, "I have felt more unwell than usual and my head aches a good deal and my eyes, so you must excuse me if I don't write much."[10]

In a cheerful mood when she was in the middle of her thirty-seventh year, she wrote to her Hartford friend, Georgiana May, "I like to grow old and have six children and cares endless."[11] But a few months later her youngest child was dead, and a year later she was pregnant once again, delivering her last child when she was thirty-nine.

Mourning is expressed, of course, according to the culture. In ancient times, infant deaths were not even recorded accurately. Suetonius, for example, merely mentions that a couple had "several" children, "of whom three survived."[12]

Among the Victorians, death was a frequent visitor, as it had been among their forebears, but the middle class made a cult of it as their parents had not. Their mourning customs were elaborate. These included little benches in cemeteries, decorated vaults, weeping willows, and the endless samplers turned out by girls and women as mourning pieces. They kept the hair of the dead person (like the locks given away by the dying Eva) entwined with dried flowers and leaves. Many nineteenth-century coffins were custom-made. The wake was held at home. After the funeral and for a year or more, close survivors usually visited the loved one's grave at least once a week. Elizabeth Cady accompanied her father to the grave of his dead son—her brother—week after week, and Harriet and Calvin Stowe mourned together at his first wife's grave in Cincinnati.

In real life and in novels, the deathbed scene was a major one. In a long novel there might be several such scenes; the deaths of Eva and Uncle Tom are among the most prolonged scenes in the book. And deaths usually took place at home, not, as today, in a hospital or nursing home. Of Mark Twain's four children, three died before him, all at home: his infant son from diptheria; a daughter from spinal meningitis; and another daughter from drowning during an epileptic seizure. His beautiful home in Hartford thus held too many painful memories for him, and these, as well as his financial problems, caused him to abandon the house.

The modern reader tends to prefer starkness in descriptions of death, and Harriet Stowe's sentimental account of the dying Eva, who gives away neat locks of hair and exhibits no repulsive symptoms of illness, seems to the modern reader perhaps overdone. But Eva was a child and so was treated gently by Stowe, unlike old Prue, whom the flies "got to."

Disease and death were not only the common visitors they always had been, but they were also publicized visitors, in an age of cheap printing; and they appeared to a middle class prosperous enough and with time enough to contemplate at length the horrors of living.

We have seen that many books written by physicians included frightening passages on female ailments, and these were written for, and read by, not physicians, but middle-class women. Some accounts were bizarre.

One chapter in *The Glory of Women* of 1896 is entitled "Pregnancy External to the Womb," and it includes a gruesome drawing of a fully formed fetus growing outside the womb. The horror story includes a description of a fetus allegedly passed through the rectum. "Should any of the bones, in their passage through the rectum, become fixed in that bowel, which is very likely to happen with the broad bones of the skull, the femur and some others, they may be carefully removed, either by the fingers, or a pair of forceps."[13]

That such an unlikely event should be included in a book for lay readers is an example of the insensitivity and unreliability of many medical authors. The terror of a young expectant mother reading the chapter can only be imagined.

That there was basis for "real" fear because of being female is quite clear. There is also no doubt that middle-class Victorian women were preoccupied with their bodies. The cult of the bath, both at home and at water-cure establishments, was extensive.

Catharine Beecher visted more than thirteen water-cure establishments. In her *Physiology and Calisthenics for Schools and Families*, there is a large appendix entitled "Water-Cure Treatment for Families." And in Mrs. Ellet's popular *Cyclopedia*, a large listing of bath therapies is given—among them sitz baths, leg baths, and foot baths. Cold water is recommended in the summer, tepid water in the winter.

About the bodies of women there grew lore both frightening and bizarre. It made women painfully self-conscious, and since doctors were now regarded as major authority figures on many subjects, women accepted the pronouncements. For example, it was said that a woman gave off an odor, a "parfum de

femme," according to the color of her hair, with redheads having the strongest perfume. A virgin exuded a very special fra-
grance, which changed when she fell in love! At the time of
menstruation "the woman's respiration has the odor of onions."[14] There were no books published about male odors.

Not all female odors were presented as seductive. At menopause, flatulence allegedly prevailed, making the woman repulsive. Gynecological treatments were painful. Until about
1880, infections of the uterus and vagina were treated with
injections of assorted substances ranging from milk to tea.
Cauterization with nitrate of silver, which burned tissue, was
usual. Leeches were occasionally prescribed for bleeding.
Depression over the "flowing to death" during menopause was
felt by Isabella Hooker.[15]

Was all of Victorian America a gigantic sickroom for women?
Of course not, although the survey by Catharine Beecher in
1855 produced some dismal responses. In the course of her
lecturing, she traveled to many cities, and she declared that
her survey included women in "almost all the Free States."
Each of her correspondents was asked to list the ten married
women she knew best and to describe their health with choices
of "perfectly healthy, well, sick or invalid." About forty per
cent of women reported were described as feeble or invalid;
the most usual complaints were "pelvic disorder" and "head-
ache." Catharine herself, in the mixture of subjectivity and
objectivity so common in Victorian surveys, declared that of
her nine married sisters and sisters-in-law, all of them except
two were either "delicate" or "invalid." If marriage and motherhood were as important and as satisfying as men declared,
why were there so many invalid and depressed wives?

It is useful to consider at what point individual pathology
becomes prevalent enough to suggest cultural pathology. One
of the most productive ways of examining the question is to
look at the phenomenon of hysteria in the Victorian period, a
subject that is receiving considerable current attention.

In a study of the hysteric, Carroll Smith-Rosenberg notes
"the existence in virtually every era of Western culture of some
clinical entity called hysteria."[16] The reader of Shakespeare's
King Lear remembers the *hysterica passio*, the hysterical suf-

fering of the King as he suffers from the unfilial behavior of his daughters. Thus males too can experience hysteria.

Yet the prevalence of hysteria among women in the nineteenth century suggests that it provided a role for many women. It attracted attention; it made others take the afflicted woman seriously. Even when physicians wondered whether hysteria was a true illness or merely "ideational" (functional—as we would call it today), they had to recognize the patient as a person in distress. But the symptoms often were not tidy; for example, paralysis of a limb would move from one limb to another.

For many decades, a fit or seizure was the determining clinical feature for the diagnosis of hysteria, but later in the century "the hysterical female character" gradually was recognized in nineteenth-century medical literature. The hysteric was regarded as "highly impressionistic, suggestible, and narcissistic."[17]

Although physicians recognized similar symptoms in men, they noted that most incidents occurred in women between puberty and menopause. This is a very long period, indeed, and obviously represents a woman's reproductive span.

There were two principal treatments for the hysterical woman. One was based on force and fear: the woman might be soaked in cold water, slapped, or given a sermon. The second method was also based upon a male authority figure, but it was the iron hand in a velvet glove. Here the patient was encouraged to please her physician. Dr. S. Weir Mitchell of Philadelphia designed a rest cure that included massage, forced feeding, and total submission to his regimen.

In the middle class, there were strict rules for wives, given authoritatively by physicians as well as writers on etiquette, for physicians regarded themselves as authorities on virtually everything! Thus, in the "medical" book, *Glory of Woman*, there are such unmedical exhortations as this: "Woman should do her best to retain those loving ways and manners by which she first drew forth a husband's love, and those who are loved least should try hardest."[18]

It seemed not to occur to physicians that if young girls were brought up to be passive, gentle, and affectionate, to please and to weep, rather than to be assertive and critical, many of them—not all of them—under conditions of stress as women would slip back, would regress, into childlike behavior. When girls and young women were exhorted by both parents to be good, and by such authoritative-sounding women as Catharine Beecher to adopt a saintly approach to marriage and motherhood, they might indeed feel worthless after lapses from good behavior. And not having developed any ego-strength, a woman might drift into hysteria or semi-invalidism. There is no question, of course, as has been noted, that much of female invalidism was real.

What did average physicians prescribe as home remedies? Exercise, but in moderation. A favorite print of the time shows women ice-skating, nicely balanced in spite of the fact that their waists are nipped in by corsets, their skirts are long and cumbersome, their heads are covered not by sensible knitted hats, but by elegant concoctions of ribbon and plumes, presumably held on with a hundred hatpins!

Surely there were depressed men, but as a sex most men knew they had more power than women, and they liked it. Women were expected to respond to men's needs and to repress their own. If a woman enjoyed sexual activity, she might be called lascivious. Dr. Bernard Talmey was speaking presumably not only as a gynecologist but as a moralist when he declared, " . . . in the long run, a man dislikes a lascivious woman. What he wishes is a modest woman who never asks for conjugal embrace when he is not disposed to it, and at times even knows how to gently and tactfully refuse her favors." [19]

Yet physician Dr. William Goodell was incensed by "pallid" women who disliked sexual expression. Thus, there was no uniform message that an anxious young woman could find; each message was given by an authoritative male voice, but the voices didn't agree.

When in doubt, gentleness and passivity were safe. In a short story, *The Yellow Wall-Paper*, by Charlotte Perkins Gilman (1892), the protagonist is a physician's wife who suffers from a psychotic depression. She has a young child, but in her depressed state, the child loses meaning for her. The authoritarian, yet polite, husband, who comes and goes in his busy rounds, addresses her as "little girl." By the end of the story, the wife has moved completely into her own private world, creeping about the room with the yellow wall-paper; paper that she later strips off in order to free the fantasied imprisoned woman living behind the paper. Her final words are "I've gotten out at last."[20]

For a superb example of a real woman obliged to live in a real sickroom, Alice James should be considered. Her brother Henry was tremendously interested in young victims of the upper class. His ideal woman-martyrs always waste away without grossness. In real life, the dying of his young cousin, Minny (Mary) Temple, provided him with a model worthy of being idealized. She possessed for him "all that wonderful ethereal brightness of presence." She "never seemed to have come into this world for her own happiness—as that of others—or as anything but as a sort of divine reminder and quickness—a transcendent protest against our acquiescence in its grossness."[21]

Henry's sister, Alice, by contrast, had little of the transcendent. She at first retreated into invalidism as a defense against anger, but later grew to know herself while on a real sickbed. She embodied the paradox of an "imaginary invalid" who became a real invalid suffering with cancer, a woman who moved from hysteria and fainting spells in her early years to considerable courage and even wit in dealing with her approaching death from cancer.

Her dear friend and live-in companion, Katharine Peabody Loring, whom Alice, at the age of thirty-two, came to know, furnished her not only tenderness during her illness but a trenchant and funny commentary on the ways of the world. When Alice was frustrated and sometimes in pain during her illness, she thought, and finally said, the word "Damn!"—a word recommended by Katharine, but a word "denied with her other rights to *Woman*."[22] Alice declared: "How sick one gets of being 'good,' how much I should respect myself if I could burst out and make every one wretched for 24 hours; embody selfishness. . . ."[23]

William, the psychologist-scientist, was relatively cool about his sister's dying; since she had been much frustrated in life, he speculated, it probably wasn't worth living for her. "You can't tell how I've pitied you," he wrote in 1891.[24]

However, Alice found life, as it slowly slipped from her, very interesting indeed, and occasionally even amusing. Surrounded by charwomen and their extended families, she saw them as part of the human comedy. She mused in June of 1889, a month after she began the diary that she would continue until her death, "I wonder if it is indelicate for a flaccid virgin to be so preoccupied with the multiplication of the species, but it fairly haunts me. . . . "[25]

She had ample opportunity to hear about "multiplication of the species" as her household workers and attendants talked about their enormous families. With humor almost Dickensian, she wrote in her diary about the father of one large family, "Imagine being personally responsible for the cutting of 800 teeth!"[26]

Toward the end of her life, she was able to develop a good self-image. Perhaps she had always been aware of possessing some ability, but as her brother Henry commented, "In our family group girls seem scarcely to have had a chance."[27]

As the only daughter in a family of four sons, she might have expected to receive much attention. Indeed she did, during her sojourns in the sickroom. However, she also recorded such youthful fantasies as "knocking off the head of the benignant Pater. . . . "[28] Yet after the death of her mother, she looked after her father very competently. When in charge, she usually did well. Another surge of competence came during her work with benevolent associations in Boston.

But her ultimate and happiest ménage was with Ms. Loring from Beverly, Massachusetts. By then she had learned to say "Damn!" But she was aware of the rage she had suppressed: "Conceive of never being without the sense that if you let yourself go for a moment your mechanism will fall into pie. . . . "[29]

One of the most bizarre escapes from passivity was the job of the female medium. To be a medium was to have power, to stand on a public platform, to be given attention, even to take on male roles! One medium in the 1880's took the roles of

thirty-one "spirits." These included an Indian and a soldier—
all voices that were produced as the medium went into a
trancelike state.[30] Tennessee Claflin, sister of the notorious
Victoria Woodhull, appeared in a variety of roles, and was
photographed, very handsome indeed, in a man's clothing and
with short hair.

Mediums were usually small-town girls with little education and a flair for the dramatic. Often their fathers saw in
them a potential for profit. This was true of the parents of the
notorious Claflin sisters. The girls were born into a poor family in Ohio, two of ten children. They worked in medicine shows,
eventually became mediums, and through their skill and the
desire of wealthy Cornelius Vanderbilt to communicate with
his son, they became his protégées.

Spiritualism was immensely popular, particularly among
women, in both England and America. Much of its acceptance
among educated people was based on the concept of unseen
particles. The first telegraphic message sent from Washington
to Baltimore by Samuel Morse in 1844 excited many with the
idea of invisible electric particles. If unseen particles of matter existed, why not unseen particles of spirit—psychic phe-
nomena? And with death so frequent a visitor in all homes,
there was a large audience for mediums. Not always was the
spirit of the loved one demanded; strangers speaking in tongues
were acceptable too, for this "proved" an invisible life. It was
an exciting way to deal with death, far more exciting than
visits to a cemetery.

Male mediums prospered too, but female mediums outnumbered them. When the New York *Tribune* publicized the Fox
sisters and their psychic table rappings, the public was fascinated.

By 1860 there were enough mediums to justify the founding
in Boston of the Mediums Mutual Aid Association![31] Kate Fox
founded the Spiritualist Movement in Rochester, New York,
in 1849, and later was paid a retainer of $1,200 a year by a
rich industrialist in New York to give consultations to him
and his wealthy friends, who included Cornelius Vanderbilt.[32]
For ordinary mediums the usual retainer was five dollars for

an evening's work—a large sum in those times, when an average factory worker earned little more than a dollar a day.

People in important places frequented mediums or invited them to their homes, although quite often the visits were treated with secrecy. For example, Harriet Stowe placed a postscript in a letter to William Lloyd Garrison, the famous Abolitionist, a reminder to write to her of a "Spiritual experience" he had mentioned to her.[33] Her sister Isabella kept a secret diary of spiritualistic experiences. Even Mrs. Lincoln employed one Cora Maynard as her favorite medium. Maynard, proud of her vocation, described herself as "an unlettered girl" who was "the honored guest of the Ruler of our Great Nation during the most memorable events in its histories."[34] Victoria Claflin Woodhull went from the profession of medium to that of editor, and president of the American Association of Spiritualists. But her hope for Spiritualism went far beyond the usual sessions of clairvoyance: "My idea and hope for modern Spiritualism is that it shall become the Religion of Humanity," she declared.[35] She was anticlerical, anti-Establishment, and she viewed spiritualism as a liberating movement that placed both men and women in a larger world than the closed world of sexual repression maintained by power politics. For Alice James, however, spiritualism was for "curious, spongy minds that sop it all up and lose all sense of taste and humour!"[36]

On the one hand it can be said that the Victorian female was an ideal person to be a medium, for, having no identity of her own, she found it relatively easy to assume the identity of another! However, most mediums were aggressive women who found the vocation one that satisfied their wish for attention and that provided a relatively good income.

Above all, it provided freedom: to travel, to be relatively free of normal conventions governing women's behavior. They liked the role reversal. The divorced husband of the medium Cora Richmond asserted that of three hundred married mediums in the Northern states about whom he had information, "half had dissolved their conjugal relations."[37]

However exotic it might have seemed to live as a medium,

it was hardly an occupation that most women could adopt! And only so much ice-skating could be done in winter, only so many sitz baths sat in at water-cure establishments and at home! What other methods were practiced by a married woman with sufficient leisure to cope with the stresses of her role? If she was poor, of course, she had to find a job.

With enough money she could become an insatiable consumer. Charlotte Perkins Gilman in 1898 said bluntly: "Women consume economic goods."[38] In Anna Mowatt's play *Fashion*, first presented in 1845 and revived many times thereafter, women with money are presented comically, as avid consumers eager to marry off their daughters to prestigious suitors.

Mrs. Tiffany is a former milliner whose merchant-husband has prospered. She uses French phrases, which she always mispronounces, changes the name of her black houseman from Zeke (too ordinary) to Adolph, and encourages a third-rate poet (she cares nothing for poetry) to call. She tries to marry her daughter to a Count, only to learn that he has been only a valet and a pastry cook in his native land! Finally she is forced to confront her own stupidity and pretentiousness. Two sterling persons fortunately are also in the household as visitors. One of them, Mr. Trueman, reveals the truth and also saves the Tiffany family from the threats of a blackmailer.

Mrs. Tiffany is portrayed as a grandiose person: she gives balls and pays hundreds of dollars for a gown. Meanwhile a seamstress is paid fifty cents for an entire mantle!

Fashion is a comedy in which common sense finally prevails, but the play does expose the dark side of nineteenth-century capitalism, the side that later prompted Catharine Beecher to ask with anger how a truly Christian people could spend so much money on themselves and their pleasures while ignoring the misery and poverty of their fellows.

Such newly rich as Mrs. Tiffany were criticized by women writers like popular Mrs. Ellet, sure of a market among wealthy and middle-class readers. Her book entitled *The Queens of American Society* was in its sixth edition in 1873. The goal of the book is to present American matrons so distinguished in the republic that they are worthy of belonging to any aristocracy.

Mrs. Ellet firmly disassociated herself and her "queens" from the newly rich who arose after the Civil War.

> Since the condition of things during the war enabled men to amass fortunes in an incredibly short time, and the discovery of oil in almost worthless lands gave them suddenly immense value, the "shoddy" and "petroleum" element has been prominent in circles composed of wealthy persons inclined to scatter their money profusely for the purpose of display. These leaders of gayety flutter in the admiring gaze of the stupid and ignorant masses, but they are not worthy to be named in the same category with those who can boast better claims to distinction than merely the possession of money.[39]

During the season of 1865–66, Mrs. Ellet said, "six hundred balls, more or less public" were given in New York City. She added, "Frequently ten thousand dollars might be seen glittering on one fine form: the cost having increased since diamond dust became a necessity in a lady's toilet."

In spite of Mrs. Ellet's scorn of the newly rich, her description of the ball given by Mrs. William Schermerhorn, a dowager of whom Mrs. Ellet is in awe, suggests as much conspicuous display of finery and self-satisfaction as found in any party given by the newly rich.

> She gave three of the most splendid receptions in the city in the winter of 1867 . . . a famous bal costume de rigueur, illustrating the reign of Louis XV . . . six hundred guests were invited; all of whom came dressed in the prescribed costume. The dresses, exclusive of jewelry were said to have cost between forty and fifty thousand dollars; the jewelry over half a million. The servants were dressed in the uniform of the period.[40]

The American aristocrats depicted in such novels as Edith Wharton's *The Age of Innocence* are far more elegant than Mrs. Schermerhorn's friends. They do not believe in conspicuous consumption. They move graciously from drawing rooms and private balls in New York to mansions on the Hudson, and to settings in Florida. (Even thrifty Harriet Beecher Stowe bought a house in Mandarin, Florida.)

But in the world of Wharton, the world of inherited money and emphasis on good manners, there also exists hypocrisy. Such matters as adultery are dealt with discreetly. To the well-bred Wharton set, the scandal involving the Reverend Henry Ward Beecher and Elizabeth Tilton (Mrs. Theodore), wife of a parishioner, would have been distasteful not only because of the adultery, but because of a trial of almost six months, and the vulgar publicity that surrounded the affair, which was stirred and kept hot by family, friends, and, above all, by journalists such as Victoria Woodhull.

In spite of, or partly because of, all the good manners in Wharton's world, many of the women seem smothered, and indeed their husbands wander in part because the wives are dull and lacking in spontaneity. Nevertheless, marriages in *The Age of Innocence* are usually arranged very sensibly, with the goal of uniting old names and old fortunes.

9

"THE UNMARRIED CLASS"

For a variety of reasons, many women made a decision to remain unmarried. Some remained single because there were not enough men available to be husbands: half a million men had died in the Civil War, in battle and from disease.

It is likely that many bright women chose to remain unmarried because they observed the life of a wife and mother to be beset with hazard. To launch into matrimony with the almost inevitable frequent pregnancies was for a woman to take a chance that she might prefer to avoid. For example, a record of thirty women before 1880 who had abdominal operations for intraabdominal pregnancy shows that only five survived the operation.[1]

Furthermore, if she wanted to pursue an ambition, a bright woman knew that she should not take on many ties and responsibilities. A study by Ann Douglas of thirty distinguished American women in the nineteenth century, many of whom were housewives, writers, and teachers at various times in their lives, lists twelve of the women as single, including Martha Finley, the best-selling author of books celebrating the family![2] The other women studied by Ms. Douglas were either childless although married, or had a small family. Only five women had more than three children. Most women had servants.

Some of Mary Wilkins Freeman's fictional women declare strongly for the unmarried state. (Wilkins herself married at the age of fifty.) "A Moral Exigency" is one of her most daring stories. It is concerned with female bonding as well as celibacy. Eunice, a minister's daughter, gives up the most attractive suitor in her small town primarily because she feels loyalty to a younger and weaker woman who will be far more unhappy than she at the loss of the man, who had courted both women.

Eunice's loyalty to her friend is the principal theme, but earlier in the story Freeman permits Eunice a remark that must have brought a blush to many a Victorian cheek. A proper Victorian woman was not supposed to speak bluntly about having children, or to say that she would not welcome them.

Eunice's father has been encouraging the suit of a poor widower with young children, and he reminds Eunice that she had not had any other "visitors." He says, "You would be well provided for in this way."

"Exceedingly well," replied Eunice slowly. "There would be six hundred a year and a leaky parsonage for a man and woman and four children, and nobody knows how many more."

Some wives, particularly among the poor, were battered wives. But drunkenness in a husband, Victoria Woodhull stormed in her radical newspaper, *Woodhull and Claflin's Weekly*, was often accepted by a judge as an excuse for wife-beating. The ironic caption for a news item that she ran on June 11, 1870 was *Killing No Murder*. Yet the torture inflicted upon the wife before her death, Woodhull, wrote, would have made "Indian torture" seem "a mercy."

Woodhull was not the only reformer who railed against wife abuse. Elizabeth Cady Stanton never forgot the poor Irish women near whom she had lived. Every Saturday night was for them a beating night. As a remedy, both Stanton and Catharine Beecher, although apart in their views about woman suffrage, advocated communities based on François Fourier's phalansteries, small communes where women and their children could live safe from the brutality of men. Charlotte Perkins Gilman also suggested communities of women. In many a Victorian story, violence during drunkenness is recounted. In Crane's *Maggie*, 1893, the husband and wife when drunk beat each other and their children as well.

Early in her marriage, Stanton cast a compassionate eye on women living in the village near her, but less fortunate than herself, Irish immigrant women worn out with toil and often brutalized by men.

> Alas! Alas! who can measure the mountain of sorrow and suffering endured in unwelcome motherhood in the abodes of ignorance, poverty, and vice, where terror-stricken women and children are the victims of strong men frenzied with passion and intoxicating drink?[3]

It was fear and anger about the violence triggered by alcohol that led to the formation of the Women's Christian Temperance Union (WCTU) in 1874. The Union was important also as a way of creating a feeling of sisterhood at a time when the woman's suffrage movement was divided by quarrels among its leaders. The temperance movement began with roots-and-branches groups all over the country whose aim was to close down the many saloons that lined the streets, especially in poor neighborhoods.

The movement produced distinguished women leaders; most outstanding was Frances Willard, who never married. She was at first a teacher and head of a woman's college, then president of the Illinois chapter of the WCTU. In 1879 she became the national president. She and her cohorts closed down three thousand saloons in six months. It was Willard who added woman suffrage to WCTU's goals.[4] Even though only men could vote, women members agreed to serve food at the polls to the voters, simply to get public attention for their cause! By 1892 WCTU's membership was almost a quarter of a million women, and it included a lively program for young people.

It is not surprising that some women throve as widows. The sense of freedom felt by one widow, a maverick, is expressed in Kate Chopin's "The Dream of an Hour," one of more than a hundred stories she wrote in eight years. The story presents a woman who has just learned of the death of her husband in a railroad accident. She weeps, then shuts herself in her room.

> She knew that she would weep again when she saw the kind, tender hands folded in death. . . . But she saw beyond that

bitter moment a long procession of years to come that would belong to her absolutely. And she opened and spread her arms out to them in welcome.

Her husband has not been cruel to her; she remembers that his hands are "kind and tender." But she yearns for her liberty. Therefore, when she opens her bedroom door to a knock and sees her husband standing there (the news of his death has been greatly exaggerated), she dies, dies of a heart attack, "of joy that kills," as the doctors interpret it. The reader understands, however, what her feelings really were.

For the very poor woman with many young children, widowhood was a terror because the breadwinner was dead and there was no one to look after the children. Such private charities as existed were rather haphazard. But for widows who inherited large estates, widowhood could be a time of blooming, and an opportunity, if they chose it, for ennobling the reputation of the dead spouse.

Such was the case for Mrs. Samuel Colt, the widow of the firearms king, who, like Queen Victoria, long outlived her husband. He died in 1862; she lived until 1905, and enjoyed an income of $200,000 a year in an age before income tax. She grieved at the loss of her children; only one of the five survived infancy. Yet Elizabeth Jarvis Colt reigned as a dowager queen. When her only surviving son, Caldwell, became twenty-one, she gave a gala party that was one of the great events of the city's social life. When her sister married, she gave a reception for a thousand guests.[5]

After her husband died, she had a church built in his honor, with the Colt firearms immortalized in stained glass. After her wastrel son died, she commemorated his love of sailing. She also commissioned a tactful author to write a biography that ennobled her husband. History, she was determined, would be controlled by herself, as much as she was able. Harriet Beecher Stowe felt the same way when she asked her son, Charles, to write the story of her life. Then she edited his work.

Elizabeth Jarvis Colt, a widow living on a tax-free income of almost a quarter of a million dollars a year, looked out on her manor in the city, with its square mile of grounds and a half-mile of greenhouses; doubtless she found life often good. She had long finished with marriage and childbearing and had furnished her life with good works, as well as material objects.

10

THE "FRAGILE" BODY AT WORK IN FACTORY, FARM, AND HOME

By 1900, about five million women, or twenty per cent of females over the age of ten, were in the American labor force.[1] The number of employed women was three times what it had been thirty years before.

Domestic work and personal service accounted for forty per cent of the jobs of women and girls—down from seventy per cent in 1870. However, many nurses were classified as in domestic service, along with women in restaurants and hotel work. In those days, "domestic service" was a broad category.

Eighty-five per cent of working women were single, and most of them lived at home. They tended to work for a few years and then to marry and leave their jobs. In New York City, the YWCA was established in 1870 to provide decent accommodations for women. However, married "sweaters," the women who did piecework at home—rolling cigars, sewing garments, for example—were able to keep an eye on their children in the tenements while earning small amounts of money at the same time.

A hundred years ago the average age of a woman worker was twenty-three, and she usually began work at about the age of fifteen. Her work week, like the work week for males, was fifty hours or more. Most women workers were native-born, but eight per cent of them had foreign-born parents. It is interesting that the jobs of the urban poor in the 1920's, described by Michael Gold in *Jews Without Money* (1930), were the same kind of jobs of the poor in the 1890's. Gold reports the misery of the "sweater." These men and women lived and worked in a tenement room and were totally dependent upon piecework brought in to be finished. A typical sweater rented her sewing machine from the man who supplied the piecework. If she became sick, or demand for her work dropped off, the machine was repossessed.

The latter half of the century saw the founding of many benevolent associations, particularly those which helped the urban poor. The Salvation Army, founded by "General" William Booth, a Methodist minister, was established in the United States in 1880. The Young Men's Christian Association was founded as early as 1844, and by 1853 included facilities for blacks, usually separate. Jewish philanthropists also made donations. In 1853 in New York the Children's Aid Society was founded. In addition, both cities and towns had poorhouses to which the destitute were sent. Some of the elderly poor, like the two old women described by Mary Wilkins Freeman in "A Mistaken Charity," were too proud to live in an alms-house.

The men who laid the railroad tracks in New England lived with their families in shelters worse than those of the horses owned by Yankee townspeople. A horrified account was published in *The New England Weekly Gazette* on February 24, 1849.

> After viewing the road, we went down below to take a look at the "hotels" alias "shanties" of the laborers who work here. Into several of these hovels we entered. Such misery, such squallor [sic], such utter wretchedness, such absence of everything calculated to make life tolerable . . . we never before beheld. . . . In a board shantie some ten to twelve feet square, there will be huddled a dozen persons, many of them without a coat, the children without a shadow of a shoe or stocking. . . . Dirt and filth are household companions of the men and women. Many an owner would hesitate about quartering his horse in such a hole; many a horse has a cleaner, sweeter beding [sic] place assigned to him. Ignorant and degraded, the emigrants seem sunk almost to the level of brutes.[2]

In the cities, the distribution of their resources by charitable organizations was often haphazard and inefficient. In Hartford, Connecticut, it was not until 1880 that a "Board of Organized Charity" was finally incorporated by the General Assembly and registration required from those who received assistance from the "almoners," the ancestors of social workers. Previously there had been duplication of services for some clients and complete deprivation of services for others.

Both board members and paid managers of charitable organizations wanted to be sure that their clients were the deserving poor, not the lazy. Their problem was summed up by one settlement-house officer in 1878 in Hartford: "How to assist the able-bodied who are out of work, perhaps only temporarily, without setting a premium upon idleness, is a question to harass the most sagacious."[3]

In the cities a strong man was seldom without a chance for a job, a job at hard labor. The cobblestone streets were laid by hand, the stone chipped and finished by hand. In mill towns where jobs were in heavy industry, the work load was brutal. The almost-forgotten story of Rebecca Harding Davis, "Life in the Iron Mills," gives a vivid account of the lives of two iron-mill workers, in Wheeling, (then) Virginia, in 1861. "Their lives . . . incessant labor, sleeping in kennel-like rooms, eating rank pork and molasses, drinking—God and the distillers only know what; with an occasional night in jail, to atone for some drunken excess."[4]

The hard lives of the working poor in New York City described by Jacob Riis in *How the Other Half Lives*, published in 1890, are not lives devoted to heavy manual labor, like the stirring and pouring of molten iron. They are lives in which there is no dividing line between home and work, because the work, concentrated small motions of sewing or making cigars, is done at home by workers for "sweaters," who own or rent out materials, whether clothing or tobacco leaves.

Riis, an investigative police reporter, described the sweatshop workers in an East Side tenement. They worked at six rented sewing machines in one flat and paid two dollars a month for the use of each machine, turning out 120 dozen "knee-pants" in a week. (In those days boys wore knee-pants or knickers, not long pants.) The workers were paid seventy cents for each dozen pairs of pants.

Food was cheap relative to wages; a quart of milk cost only four cents. But rents were high in the cities; a typical two-room flat rented for twenty dollars a month. And there was no job security. Work could never be counted on and, therefore, was seized when it was available, no matter how outrageously low the wages.

The tailors and seamstresses were not alone in being exploited. Riis describes a Bohemian couple, a man and wife who were able to finish three thousand cigars in a week; the tobacco leaves were supplied by the jobber. The couple was paid $3.75 per thousand cigars. They often labored until midnight.[5]

Catharine Beecher, reporting the information given her by a missionary in New York City, which in 1860 already had a population of a million, gave some horrifying statistics:

> 290,000 inhabitants to a square mile in the Fourth Ward;
> half the houses with no drain or connection to a sewer, the liquid refuse is emptied on the sidewalk or into the street; in one "tenant-house" 146 persons sick with "small-pox, typhus fever, scarlatina, measles, marasmus, phthisis pulmonales [tuberculosis], dysentery, and chronic diarrhea."[6]

Vaccination against smallpox was known; Pasteur had published about microorganisms. Every educated person knew that efficient drains and sewers were needed. But the spread of knowledge was slow, and there was little incentive in government and in the general public to carry out the reforms possible after scientific discoveries.

Cholera and tuberculosis were rampant. Although in New York City by 1890 the drinking water was relatively safe for the enormous population of a million and a half, the crowded conditions—several people in one small room, many tenements, back to back and side to side—encouraged the spread of disease. Riis estimated that there were "twelve hundred thousand" tenement dwellers in New York City.[7] In two tenements he surveyed, there lived 180 children.[8]

The death rate for children in the tenements was over fifty per cent. In "the Bend," a notorious slum neighborhood, sixty-eight per cent of the deaths on one block were of children, a figure worse than that in Colonial times.[9] As Riis said, the measles that went "lightly on the avenue" was a killer in the tenements. Abandoned infants died in the streets. Of 508 infants received at the Randall's Island Hospital in 1889, 333 died. One hundred and seventy of these were picked up from the streets; the others were born in hospitals.[10] According to Riis, in Potter's Field, the bodies of adults were piled "three stories deep, shoulder to shoulder . . . to save space."[11]

So many mothers left their babies in the doorway of the Foundling Asylum of the Sisters of Charity on 68th Street under the open-door policy, that the Sisters changed the rules and required a mother to appear in person and also to consent to breastfeed an abandoned foundling as well as her own child.[12] Some parents took insurance policies on the lives of their infants for five to twenty-five cents a week premium, eager for benefits at the death of the child.[13] Riis was appalled.

Riis estimated that an average of eight million dollars was spent annually by public and private charities in New York City. But the number of needy persons far outnumbered the resources offered. In addition to the blind and the halt and the orphans, there were the drunken, estimated by Riis, who took some photographs of their doomed selves, to run as high as forty per cent among paupers. Riis stated that there were in New York City below 14th Street approximately 111 chapels and churches versus more than four thousand saloons.[14] In addition, there were the informal "gin mills and beer joints" where minors were often served beer. A sensational story about a boy drunk with beer and "killed and half-eaten by rats" was published in the newspapers.[15] An investigation was made, then interest cooled, and business went on as usual.

The mentally ill were crowded together unless they were able to enter a private hospital. On Blackwell's Island, where seventeen hundred mentally ill women were housed, the women were roped together when they were taken out for their after-noon walk, so that they would not jump or fall into the river.[16] On Ward's Island, where the male patients were housed, life was as dreary.

Riis pointed out that greedy slumlords demanded a fifteen to thirty per cent return on their capital, whereas a minority of decent landlords was content with five per cent.[17] The devious "complied" by fakery with the safety standards enacted in 1869; tenement owners were required to provide airshafts for light and ventilation, and fire escapes, but some landlords allowed fire escapes to terminate in places where there was no exit from inside the building! As for the jobber who paid the sweaters, the markup of the product was close to one hundred per cent. For example, a Bowery firm sold fifteen thousand suits at $1.95 each; the total cost to them per suit was $1.12.[18]

It would seem that the sweater had the most hideous of jobs, but there were seemingly attractive jobs that turned out also to be exhausting. The young "cash girls," retail clerks, who gave their age as fourteen, the legal age for work, but who often were younger, worked sixteen hours a day in holi-day seasons. They were expected to stay on their feet and were fined for sitting down. Since the supervisors received a percentage of the fines, they were motivated to be zealots. The cash girl averaged two dollars a week in wages and paid about $1.50 a week for her room.

The cash girl, in her relatively exotic workplace, and the female laundry worker, at washtub or ironing board, had in common a long week of standing on their feet, at two dollars a week; but at least the laundry workers became unionized in 1866 and improved their wages to eight dollars a week or more.[19] Working hours in mills and factories often ran to fifty-eight hours, even at the turn of the century.[20]

As more complex machines and interchangeable parts were invented, more women needing less training and experience found jobs available. Because women were willing to work for lower pay and were willing to be used as strikebreakers, they were resented and often despised by male workers. By the turn of the century, thirty-eight of one hundred workers in the tobacco industry were women, because they agreed to work for lower wages than men. In the printing trades "in several strikes local unions had been defeated by women strikebreakers."[21]

Small wonder that most labor unions wanted to exclude women as members, and as delegates to conventions. Susan Anthony was rejected at the 1869 convention of the National Labor Union "because she was not a representative of a 'bona fide' trade-union organization."[22] Yet some male delegates were not trade-union members.

The Knights of Labor, which admitted women in 1881, was hospitable to ambitious women. Leonora Barry was an effective organizer and was taken seriously. But even Barry after her marriage disappeared from power, as a witty male colleague had predicted in 1890 that she would. She was to marry a man named "Lake." "She has not yet been called across the dark river but she will soon be buried in the bosom of a Lake that shall wash away all claim that we may have to her."[23]

"Buried in the bosom" was not, however, the choice of the militant Mary Harris "Mother" Jones (1837–1930), an Irish immigrant who married, became a Socialist, and who organized miners and railroad workers. She was a friend of Terence Powderly of the Knights of Labor. She stated before a House committee in Washington, ". . . wherever a fight is on against wrong, I am always there."[24]

During the Civil War and afterwards, many women worked for the first time outside the house. A half million men were no longer in the job market after the deaths and injuries of war. But the new women workers tended to be timid. In fact, the Working Women's Protective Union in New York City was sponsored less by women than by a liberal newspaper and a few businessmen. So fearful were the women that they included in their Constitution the words, "Our object is not to molest or annoy employers"![25]

Similar unions were formed in other cities, but their lives were relatively short—about a decade—and their procedures were tentative rather than firm. Women simply were not taken seriously until they developed the confidence to go on strike and hold their position. In 1909 the thirteen-week strike of shirtwaist-makers showed the public that women had the courage to continue picketing even when harassed by company guards and New York City policemen. Six hundred women strikers were arrested. Furthermore, native-born workers, who often looked down on immigrant workers, this time joined in sympathy and observed the picket lines. Of the thirty thousand shirtmakers, about one-third were native-born Americans. Most of the others were Russian-Jewish women. Their strike was successful, and led to 312 shops becoming union shops.[26]

For many jobs, particularly those in the railroads, where pay scales were generally higher than pay scales in factories, women were never even considered. A railroad mechanic or brakeman was paid $2.50 a day, then regarded as a good wage, but women were never considered for these occupations, as they still are not today. In jobs in which both sexes performed virtually the same tasks, women were often pushed harder. It is clear from an account of work in a pickle factory in Pittsburgh at the turn of the century that women workers were expected to do more menial tasks than the men. For example, at the end of the day and the week, women workers were required to get down on their knees and use rags and scrubbing brush to clean up the sticky pickle juice, whereas men workers on another floor were allowed to use mops![27] In the case of cash girls, as Jacob Riis noted, even when their daily sales were higher than those of male clerks, they still received two dollars a week as contrasted with the male clerk's fifteen dollars.[28]

Throughout the century occupational hazards were numerous for both men and women. The spectre of "consumption" which haunted crowded dwellings was particularly evident in cotton and paper mills. The lint-filled workrooms were powerfully described by Herman Melville in a sketch published in *Harper's* in 1855. There were no major reforms in air quality in such factories until well after 1900.

Earlier, in the 1840's, life in the cotton and woolen mills along the Merrimack River in Massachusetts had been portrayed in illustrations as attractive to rosy-cheeked farm girls, who skated on the frozen river to their factory jobs. They did not remain rosy-cheeked very long.

A major protest by women workers to the Massachusetts Special Committee led to an investigation of working conditions in the mills in Lowell in 1848.[29] The Committee found the factory air "not wholesome; 293 small lamps and 61 large lamps burned in the closed working rooms during the dim hours of early morning and the dark hours of the late afternoon and night." At that time the working day began at five in the morning and usually ended at seven at night, with time for breakfast and dinner. The average wage was from $25 to $30 a month. The average worker stayed three years and was often in poor health. When the women petitioned the Massachusetts Legislature for a ten-hour day, they were considered radical.

Herman Melville's article of 1855 describes an atmosphere of drifting white particles of lint in a New England paper mill. The white particles coated the skin and clothing and entered the lungs of the workers, most of whom were women. The sketch is called "The Tartarus of Maids," and is a living legend of women turned into white pillars. A more homely comparison is to imagine breathing in each day the contents of a can of cream of tartar or baking powder.

> Nothing was heard but the low, steady overruling hum of the iron animals. The human voice was banished from the spot. Machinery—that vaunted slave of humanity—here stood menially served by human beings. . . . The girls did not seem so much accessory wheels to the general machinery as mere cogs in the wheels. . . . The air swam with the fine, poisonous particles, which from all sides darted, subtiley, as motes in sunbeams, into the lungs.[30]

Melville had the dark imagination to foresee that the machine, instead of being the servant, would become the master. He noticed also that the overseer referred to all the female employees, even older women, as "girls" (as the black man used to be called "boy"). The narrator asked the overseer, "Why is it, sir, that in most factories female operatives, of whatever age, are indiscriminately called girls, never women?" The overseer replied that no *married* women were employed; hence-everyone was a "girl" regardless of age!

And, of course, if consumption or other illness developed from working conditions, there was no sick pay. Family, friends, or the town or city might help, but no employer was required to contribute. Well into the twentieth century, working conditions in textile mills helped women to early graves, largely because of tuberculosis, to which textile workers were especially vulnerable. Dr. Arthur Perry investigated the causes of all deaths in persons from ten to forty-four years of age in the years 1905–1907 in Fall River, Massachusetts; Manchester, New Hampshire; and Pawtucket, Rhode Island. He then classified the deceased into mill operatives and non-mill operatives. He published his results as "Causes of Death Among Woman and Child Cotton Mill Operatives"—these being the two groups most poorly paid and, therefore, most employed. His major finding was that the death rate from tuberculosis among women operatives was "more than twice that of non-operatives."[31]

Life on farms for women, although hard, at least provided food, even if limited in variety. And most women after the War, including black sharecroppers, owned part of what they produced, unlike the factory or sweatshop worker who had only her labor to sell. As a black woman reported her alternatives after the Civil War, "When we-uns am given freedom, Massa . . . tells us we can stay and work for wages or share-crop the land." It was a difficult life still, but it freed black women from the demand to be breeding animals.[32]

Sarah Beaulieu, a white Wisconsin farm girl, worked her father's farm with her mother while he was in the Civil War. Part of one day's work was carrying fifty pounds of turnips from an outdoor pit.[33] But at least Sarah viewed them as *her* turnips!

Earlier in the century, farm women saved money of their own because they worked seasonally in factories, and also had small truck gardens, dairy products, and perhaps a craft specialty. For example, in Southern New England, farm women often raised a small cash crop of tobacco from which they made cigars, which they then sold in market towns.

Some of the worst exploiters of both young farm workers and young factory workers were the parents. Such a story as Hamlin Garland's "The Creamery Man" describes the immigrant daughters of the West who were worked as hard as farm animals by their parents. Males under the Homestead Act could file for 160 free acres in five years, as citizens or intended citizens, but the work of a daughter or wife in the field brought her only such return as her father or husband decided to give her. In factories, too, children were forced also to work long hours.

According to Victoria Woodhull, such exploitation was implicit in capitalism: " . . . the radically wrong thing . . . [is] the idea of ownership in human beings . . . essentially the same in the two institutions of slavery and marriage."[34] She was also appalled at the large number of prostitutes in the cities.

Dr. William Sanger, resident physician for the Blackwell's Island Women's Prison in New York City, estimated that there was one prostitute to every 52 men in the United States. His giving the statistic in such terms is itself a curiosity.

Sanger reported in a study published in 1858 that twenty-five per cent of the prostitutes he studied gave "inclination" as the cause of their becoming prostitutes;[35] Sanger defined this as a "voluntary resort to prostitution in order to gratify the sexual passions." He added that "the full force of sexual desire is seldom known to a virtuous woman." However, the actual cases that Dr. Sanger published make it clear that the prostitutes studied had been desperately poor. A former servant girl had received "one dollar a month wages." A widow with a child had earned "$1.50 a week as a tailoress." Many of the prostitutes were young, naive girls who had been seduced and then abandoned. Some of them had been abandoned by their husbands and were without jobs.

Although there was by 1900 a four hundred per cent increase in the number of manufacturing jobs held by women, domestic work accounted for more than half the working woman population. Even an ambitious young girl, as Ellen Moers points out in her account of a heroine in an adult novel by Louisa May Alcott (*Work*, 1873), had few choices.[36] Housework, therefore, was likely to be tried. In the real-life household of Harriet Beecher Stowe, a servant was paid two dollars a week and room and board. The work day began at dawn and included evenings and Sundays. Only a half-day off a week was permitted, and living-in meant almost no privacy. To these conditions most young servants objected and did not remain on the job very long. Listed in a survey as the three principal reasons for not choosing domestic work were: "Pride, social condition, and unwillingness to be called servants; confinement evenings and Sundays; more independence in other occupations."[37] The democracy of America, in spite of its limitations in 1900, encouraged most live-in servants to flee domestic work as soon as possible.

To be a shopgirl was to have freedom and some semblance of gentility, even though the average pay per week was only two dollars. A bright woman, good at spelling and nimble of finger, could find a job after the Civil War in the ever-growing ranks of secretaries. A popular goal was to be "type-writer operator." Many employers preferred fast typing to shorthand, since they could examine the dictated letter immediately.

Nursing and teaching, the two occupations that had always been considered suitable for women who needed to earn a living, continued to attract women. During the Civil War, there were not enough male nurses, and women who had formerly done only midwifery joined male nurses in the care of the sick and wounded. Some nurses, like Susie King Taylor, had no previous training. Born a slave, she worked as laundress, teacher, and finally nurse.[38] Gradually both the military and lay establishments came to tolerate female participation, although at first it was feared that dealing with such things as urinals would be too shocking for female nurses. However, prints showing the female nurse at the side of the wounded in war helped to break down segregation in nursing according to sex. She was poorly paid, however, for her services; Harriet

Tubman, who worked for three years as cook and nurse in hospitals, had to sue for back pay of $1,800.[39]

In teaching, women continued to work largely in primary school, or, if they taught adolescents, they taught girls in "female seminaries," as secondary schools for girls were called. Catharine Beecher protested against such discrimination, making the unusual chauvinistic remark that in her experience, schools taught by male teachers instead of females tended to deteriorate! She was angry also that in most colleges and universities only men were chosen as professors.[40]

As new jobs developed, both sexes sought them. Telephone operators were men, but they were later supplanted by women until recently, when males again have been recruited.

Unmarried women, or women who had raised their families, were the women with jobs. Most poor mothers with a large number of children stayed at home, or occasionally left them with the new day-care centers available in a few cities. Elizabeth Stanton was one of the fortunate—not rich, but comfortable, with two servants, a laundress, and, in the early years of her marriage, financial help from her father; so she was able to travel and lecture.

In some cities, children could be left at day-care centers organized by the settlement houses that had begun to spring up. In Hartford, Connecticut, the Union for Home Work was created by a group of rich women, including the wife of Samuel Colt, munitions maker and industrialist. While poor mothers went out and did a day's work or were taught in Union classes to use a sewing machine, their small children were looked after for ten cents a day, five cents each if more than two children attended from the same family. The children received a bath, supervision, and meals. The day began at 6:30 and ended at seven or eight at night.[41] Jane Addams' Hull House in Chicago, which received more publicity than any other settlement house in the country, also provided day-care for children and training for jobs for the mothers.

For those who had what is now known as an "extended family," there were often older women, usually unmarried relatives, who took care of the young. Harriet Stowe's Aunt, Esther Beecher, gave years of loving service to the Beecher children. She was typical of the unmarried woman who tended the children while widower or remarried father got on with his work. Aunt Esther never knew what it was to have more than a hundred dollars in cash in a year, said Harriet. Nor did Aunt Esther have her own bed, but rather shared one with a child. Having so little privacy during her life, Esther would find heaven, Harriet said, a wonderfully free and spacious place.[42]

The extended family among the well-to-do produced enclaves such as Nook Farm in Hartford, where in 1853 two men, John Hooker and his brother-in-law, Francis Gilbert, bought 140 acres. Hooker married Isabella Beecher, Harriet's half-sister; another half-sister, Mary Beecher Perkins, lived on the "Farm." Also on the property, in a cottage, was John Hooker's widowed mother. It was usual for widows to live with or near their children, and relatives were in and out of each other's house around the clock.[43] Harriet Beecher Stowe considered it not unusual even in her old age to walk several miles several times a week to visit her minister son. The practical support system, of course, for all the dining and visiting chronicled in middle-class diaries and letters, was the availability of cheaply paid servants, usually foreign-born.

Among the poor, an extended family support system was vital. In the family of Mrs. Frances Gaudet in Mississippi, who was black, her grandparents, after the death of her father during the Civil War, took responsibility for the children. Stepfathers, aunts, and uncles were all part of the support system.[44]

European immigrants clustered together for support in city tenements. Bohemian women who made cigars in New York tenements often had left their male relatives in the old country. They saved enough pennies in the new land and then paid the passage for the rest of the family. Michael Gold, writing about his family after the First World War, cites the many cousins and neighbors from the old country who settled in the same area near the port of entry. Even out West, cousinhood as portrayed in Mark Twain's *The Adventures of Huckleberry Finn* was powerful enough to enable a young roving male to find food and shelter. In fact, the final segment of the story depends upon Huck's deceiving a gullible woman into believing that he is her cousin.

Running a household in Victorian times, unless the head of the household was rich, was turned into a demanding job. The password in interior decorating among Victorians was "More." Nothing was ever simple or austere. Mantels were draped, lampshades were draped, pianos and tables were draped. Rug lay upon rug, valance upon valance: innumerable folds, pleats, and swags—two or more wallpaper patterns in the same room, plus wainscotting and dado. Middle-class woman turned consumer surrounded herself with objects requiring care.

In a well-run middle-class household nothing was supposed to be wasted. Fat was saved for soap. Tea leaves were dried to be used later for sweeping the floor; they were regarded as "settlers" of dust. Irons were heavy and kept hot on the kitchen stove, which burned wood or coal or kerosene. The furnace in the basement was stoked by a handyman in prosperous houses, and hot air came up through grates in the floor. Harriet Beecher Stowe's comfortable house in Hartford, the last one she owned, has a bathroom with a metal tub and a hot-water boiler heated by gas that can be adjusted to empty into either the tub or the washbasin. But most people used washstands in their rooms for daily washing, and the heavy slop bowls were not easy to empty or clean. Garbage disposal was a horror in the hot weather. Ash collection in snow-filled streets in winter was haphazard, and in crowded streets great mounds of ashes slid and blew about. But the middle class did not live in crowded streets. Although in apartment-hotels in New York City by the 1880's there was some central refrigeration, the vast majority of American housewives made do with chunks of ice in ice-boxes, which melted into pans that soon were coated with green slime.

Poor seamstresses worked by the light of kerosene lamps (whose wicks had to be trimmed carefully) and later by gaslight. Their clients must often have been stingy, for Lydia Sigourney, an immensely popular writer, advised in her *Whisper to a Bride*, "Be liberal to the needle-woman, who worketh late at night, by the dim lamp, while thou sleepest."[45]

The affluent but selfish housewife was much criticized by writers on household management, including minor writers as well as Harriet Beecher Stowe. (Most writers on the subject were married, since married women were regarded as more authoritative than single women.) To be a well-to-do or rich housewife was not an excuse for being lazy, according to Mrs. E. F. Ellet, one of the many writers on household management.

> The daughter of the millionaire is seldom taught to consider how great are the social responsibilities her wealth and position impose upon her,—to regard herself as a steward of the Almighty. . . . The daughters of the working class are hardly prepared for their position as wives, mothers, and housewives.[46]

It is most unlikely that Mrs. Ellet knew the daughters of any millionaires; rather her audience was the prosperous majority that believed in an enlightened capitalism. The mystique included a lower class that knew they were "working class" and a well-to-do class that accepted the role of distributor of benevolences to the worthy poor. The subheading of Mrs. Ellet's *Cyclopedia* is: "Adapted to all classes of society." The scenario is not unlike the one that was Charles Dickens's early favorite: both the deserving and undeserving poor encounter adversity, but occasionally a wealthy benefactor will turn up to rescue the deserving. Mrs. John Jacob Astor (1825–1887) was described by Jacob Riis as "that great friend of the homeless children,"[47] and Miss Ellen Collins, also his contemporary, deliberately built model tenements for the poor for a 5½ per cent profit, as contrasted with the usual landlord's profit of from fifteen to thirty per cent.[48] Collins also helped the National Freedmen's Relief Association, charged with promoting education for emancipated blacks.

The contrast in diet between the rich and the poor was extraordinary. In the late 1800's, the diet of the rich was the gout-inducing one of earlier centuries: several courses— soup, terrapin or fish, a wide choice of birds, and rich desserts. Vegetables and salad greens were in little demand. The middle class in the cities had a broad choice of fish and game; *300 Choice Receipts* collected by the ladies of Christ Church, Ansonia, Connecticut, in 1887, lists the fish and game available for each month of the year.

Listed as available and relatively cheap were no fewer than four kinds of duck—canvas-back, redhead, broadbill, and teal—as well as Scotch grouse, partridge, pheasant, woodcock, pigeons, snipe and quail. Jugged hare, that is, pickled hare, was also popular.

Beef was not much sought after. In Eastern cities, fish was popular because it was cheap; birds came next in demand. But for the very poor in the cities, the usual diet consisted of oatmeal, soup, beans, bacon, and large amounts of bread. (The manager of the settlement house in Hartford noted disapprovingly the purchase of two boxes of strawberries, for almost a dollar—a day's pay—by a poor woman who wanted something special to eat.) The diet of the urban poor was, in fact, not very different from that of the "penny stinkards" of Shakespeare's day who allegedly stank from their diet of herring and onions. The food and drink in taverns were immensely popular, of course, as Jacob Riis noted in *How the Other Half Lives*, and taverns prospered in spite of the Woman's Christian Temperance Union.

Rotten meat, although not as common as in the hot climates where curry and spices are used routinely as preservatives and maskers of overaged food, was a possibility that made most housewives and cooks suspicious when they went marketing. Most recipes that called for meat or even bones stipulated long boiling times. The beginning of a recipe for tomato soup, for example, is, "Take a shin bone, boil slowly all day.[49]

Until late in the century, the large meal of a three-meal day, for those who could afford three meals, was the midday meal, and this was a very heavy meal indeed for the middle class. It included soup, fish or meat, and a heavy dessert, often a suet-pudding or the like. The cash girl, by contrast, as Riis reported, had but one meal a day and a cup of coffee. It was all she could afford, if she rented a room, with her wages of two dollars a week. A favorite project among settlement house managers was to collect recipes for dinners that cost only fifteen cents. Later it became fashionable to have the heavy meal at the end of the day, and "lunch" at midday.

In good households, the servants ate well—probably the best enticement of domestic service. Harriet Stowe estimated that she would save two dollars a week in wages, plus another two dollars in board, if she let one domestic worker go.[50] So the cost of board was estimated to be the same amount as wages—a hundred dollars a year.

A day worker, particularly if he or she was black, did not fare as well as a live-in worker. The diet of the rural poor in the South until recent decades was mush, lard, greens, and sometimes a so-called "meat" loaf made of peanuts. For many of the rural poor, going to the city was seen as an escape from borderline subsistence. Although life in the city was seldom what the migrant hoped for, there was some attempt by private charities to help those in need, even though the assorted agencies were often inefficient and usually rivalrous. It was for these assorted groups that some of the first woman managers were recruited.

Woman managers developed, as was true also in teaching and nursing, in the helping jobs and professions. The list of settlement house managers, if all the unpublicized names were known, would be long. Jane Addams, because she was wealthy, independent, and a writer of books, came to be known as an outstanding manager. Quieter women who worked for small salaries had no one to publicize their skills. Only now are some of their diaries and account-books coming to light, after being hidden for years in basements and attics and makeshift archives in settlement houses.

Elizabeth Sluyter, Mrs. Steven Sluyter, who managed the Union for Home Work of Hartford, Connecticut, is probably typical of a woman manager employed by a wealthy and earnest board interested in helping the poor. Elizabeth Sluyter's husband, a former Captain in the Civil War, was originally hired as manager, having been asked to head a Coffee House to provide cheap food and safe drink for the poor of Hartford. For mysterious reasons, the captain did not remain manager for a very long time, and he was replaced by his wife. She became indispensable to the Union and was titled Almoner and Superintendent interchangeably.

Unlike Jane Addams, Elizabeth Sluyter did not belong to the social class that supported the settlement house. The board was a group of wealthy women who subsidized the Union for Home Work; they had met together and had done bandage-making during the Civil War, and they saw each other socially.

The Coffee House that they engaged Captain Sluyter to manage they saw as an attraction to lure the poor away from the many taverns. During the depression of 1876–77, forty thousand meals were served at the Coffee House for four cents a meal ticket, or free if the tickets came from the city missionaries or the chief of police, or the Sluyters.

Mrs. Sluyter and another settlement house manager, Mary Graham Jones, made visits to the homes of the poor and acted as ombudsmen for them. They recruited neighborhood workers as group leaders, and they struggled with the city over such practical problems as ashes and garbage collection. Said Miss Jones, "There is hardly a pound of garbage . . . that does not go into the river or on its banks."[51]

The woman managers both worked and lived in the neighborhood of the poor. Elizabeth Sluyter also raised three daughters while doing her work. In fact, she established a matriarchy, since one of her daughters succeeded her as superintendent. Such women were career persons, spending most of their adult life in their work, and training younger women as assistants.

Generally, they were poorly paid, for they worked for terms devised by a wealthy group often insensitive to the manager's needs. For example, the Samuel Colt family of Hartford was one which spent a fortune on its own pleasures and a relatively modest sum on charity. This was a typical spending pattern among the "enlightened" rich of the time. Harriet Stowe, after attending a wedding of a member of the Colt family, noted that wedding presents received by the couple were said to be worth about $25,000, a very large sum, in buying power, for that day.[52] On the other hand, Mrs. Samuel

Colt and her wealthy Board of Union for Home Work ladies paid their full-time settlement-house manager only a hundred dollars a month in salary for many years. At that rate, the woman manager, who had three daughters to support, was receiving only two dollars a day more than her average working client!

A few woman managers were political activists; in New York City, the Henry Street Settlement gave money to striking workers, and in Chicago and Hartford and other cities, both the woman managers and a few board directors considered themselves watchdogs, seeing to it that the politicians gave the poor a fair share of city services.

Most of the woman managers learned on the job. They were hired because they were diligent and bright, but there was no such thing in those days as a degree in social work, although Jane Addams went to London to learn about the new settlement-house movement in which settlement workers lived in the same neighborhood as their clients.

In the South, the plantation owner's wife participated in a larger share of social reality than was likely for the wife of the Northern industrialist or businessman. Many Southern women found themselves widow-managers of post–Civil War plantations, and after slavery was abolished, they continued to oversee workers and crops. Elizabeth Allston Pringle was one of these Southern widows.[53] She took title to her husband's rice plantation in South Carolina after his death, and her reminiscences show that her contact with the farm workers was both personal and managerial in a way impossible for the Northern industrialist's wife, who was more likely to be a sponsor of a fund-raising ball for a charitable agency than to have any sustained and direct contact with the poor.

To enter the professions of medicine and law, a woman needed a long and specialized apprenticeship. She was often rejected as an applicant to medical school, and she was often rejected by a state bar association even after years of legal experience.

Homeopathic medicine, a variety of medicine that advocates small doses of medicines for "healthy" people, was a side path that was relatively hospitable to women candidates. In 1900,

seventeen per cent of the two thousand students in homeopathic medicine were women; in regular schools of medicine,
however, only ten per cent of students were women, and most
of these went into such specialties as pediatrics or obstetrics.[54] But in the mid-1800's and for several decades afterwards, orthodox medical schools rejected women applicants.
Elizabeth Blackwell, one of the bright and aggressive Blackwell sisters, needed determination to receive the first regular
American medical degree awarded to a woman. This was
awarded in 1849 by Geneva College, later to become part of
Syracuse University. Her sister-in-law, Antoinette Brown
Blackwell, became the first ordained woman minister in the
United States.

Blackwell records the shock that the small town felt at the
sight of a *woman* medical student.[55] She supposed they thought
her either "a bad woman" or "insane." Her professors were
somewhat more sophisticated, but some told her to stay away
from their demonstrations. This "saddened and discouraged"
her. She herself found some of the dissections "just as much
as I could bear."

When she went to London for further study, a professor of
midwifery wrote her "a very polite note" saying that he "entirely disapproved of a lady's studying medicine." She pushed
on, however, noting in passing that hydrotherapy ("water-
cures") and mesmerism (a form of hypnotism), both of which
were popular on both sides of the Atlantic, were not nearly as
useful therapies as their promoters touted them to be.

When Blackwell returned to the United States, she trained
nurses, founded a separate medical college for women and a
hospital staffed entirely by women. She also crusaded against
ovariotomy or "castration" of women by removal of the ovaries. She estimated that one in every two hundred fifty European women had had the operation, and she criticized male
doctors for their encouragement of the procedure. However,
other physicians, including women, noted that women patients often requested surgical removal of the ovaries as a way
of avoiding pregnancy.

Admission of women to legal training and certification after
the training came even more slowly than did admission to

medical schools. Not until the 1890's did university law schools change their policy. However, many women learned law as assistants in law firms, insurance companies, and assorted government agencies. They were like today's paraprofessionals: competent, useful, and unlicensed.

The woman who was first admitted to the bar in Iowa, in 1869, was primarily a teacher rather than a practicing attorney; the career of Myra Colby Bradwell (1831–1894) is more to the point.[56] She studied law under her lawyer-husband's supervision, and edited and published legal materials. In 1869, she applied for admission to the state bar in Illinois, and after being refused, took her case to the Supreme Court. The Supreme Court merely denied her claim to protection under the 14th Amendment and left to the individual state the task of determining qualifications. (The 14th Amendment was the same one from which the suffragists had hoped for protection against discrimination according to sex—with equally fruitless results.)

In 1872, a sop was given to Myra Bradwell by the Illinois Bar Association when she was made an honorary member. Unappeased, she continued to work for married women's property acts, and in 1890 she had the satisfaction of having the Illinois Supreme Court act on her 1869 motion to admit her to the bar. Her triumph had taken her only twenty-one years!

Usually presidents of specialty schools and universities were cautious about what they said when they rejected a woman applicant for admission or certification. Occasionally, however, an unguarded sentence came forth that showed the bias of the administrator. The classic case is that of Belva Bennett McNall Lockwood. She was widowed at the age of twenty-three and left with a young child. She taught, studied law, later remarried, and applied for admission to the Law Department of Columbian College in Washington, D.C. She received a letter in 1869 saying that her presence "would be likely to distract the attention of the young men."[57] Undaunted, Lockwood was admitted to the new National University Law School. Ten years later she lobbied successfully in Congress in order to become the first woman permitted to practice before the Supreme Court.[58]

The letter of rejection from Columbian College reveals the ultimate sexual bias, that the female, simply because she is female, will "distract." To believe this, of course, is also to assume males to be so immature that they will respond to such "distraction."

One by one, the citadels in largely male professions were slowly opened to women, but Catharine Beecher, even in her old age, lamented that "five out of seven professors are men."[59] To be admitted into an institution at graduate level was a hard-won accomplishment, although a few undergraduate colleges early insisted on female education equivalent to male education. However, for a woman to be named a professor or a credential-awarding officer was, and remains a hundred years later, rare.

11

THE FEMINIST
NETWORK

The basic mood of feminism in the nineteenth century was not hatred of males, although there were a few female chauvinists who regarded the female body as superior to the male. For example, Eliza Farnham wrote in 1864 that the waste of sperm in male physiology implies a lack of orderliness; whereas the orderly and conservative mentrual cycle shows more efficient organization.[1] And the female brain, weighing more than the male, can be interpreted as a proof that the female is the more intelligent!

But most of the striving minority of women in the nineteenth century were not chauvinists. They wanted political and economic equality with men, and they believed that social equality would follow soon. Some, like Susan Anthony, remained unmarried. Others, like Elizabeth Cady Stanton, combined family life with political activism. She was the author of Resolution 9 (the ballot for women) of the Declaration of Sentiments in 1848, which was patterned after the Declaration of Independence. The Declaration was adopted at the Seneca Falls, New York, convention, held in a Methodist church. The convention included some men. July of 1848 is, therefore, a good date to use for the beginning of the woman's suffrage movement. Stanton, Lucretia Mott, and others wrote the call and published it in the *Seneca County Courier* the next day, "giving only five days notice."[2] The goal of the ballot would separate Stanton, Anthony, and other suffragists from such pious reformers as Catharine Beecher who saw the vote as not only a burden to women, but a device to tarnish her status. This division in perception will be examined shortly.

The support system for the women who met in Seneca Falls came from the antislavery movement. This movement, in turn, had taken nourishment from the Quakers, who from early days worshiped with blacks, although the blacks often were placed in a section of the meeting house by themselves. Some Quakers truly lived the lives dictated by their consciences. Lucretia Coffin Mott, for example, and her husband, James, gave up their prosperous cotton business in Philadelphia because they decided not to support the cotton-growing, slaveholding planters. It was Lucretia Mott who became a friend of young Elizabeth Stanton when the women attended the World Antislavery Convention in London in June 1840, where they were segregated like blacks in the meeting hall.

Originally men and women in the antislavery movement in the United States belonged to separate groups, but women later became voting members of the New England Antislavery Society and some of them went on lecture tours. The old precept that women should remain silent in public was opposed by such people as Lucretia Mott, who became a minister of the Society of Friends. Later women began to be taken seriously as they lectured against slavery. Angelina Grimké was to address fifteen hundred people in Lowell, Massachusetts. Also, the content of women's speeches broadened; Lucy Stone, as early as 1853, spoke not only against slavery and alcoholic beverages but for women's rights.

Occasionally the speakers wore the "Bloomer" costume, the familiar invention of Amelia Jenks Bloomer, founder in 1849 of *Lily*, a temperance newspaper, which soon began to publish articles on women's rights. The loose trousers, even with a skirt worn over them, shocked many in the audience. Bobbed, short hair was also frowned upon. In the audience, the average woman had long hair, carefully arranged; a well-dressed woman wore up to twenty yards of fabric.

The abolitionists were loyal to each other and had an effective network of communication, especially in New York, Boston, Philadelphia, and in such mill cities as Lowell and Lynn in Massachusetts. These antislavery workers and the suffragists shared the same turf and often became good friends. For example, the women from ten states who attended the First Antislavery Convention of American Women in New York City in 1837 formed friendships that were put to further use in the suffrage movement. Probably the most ingenious compromise in the use of time and energy was that of Lucy Stone; on weekends she worked for the American Anti-Slavery Society, and on weekdays lectured on women's rights.[3]

The shared trials and triumphs of both men and women in antislavery work led to some close-bonded marriages. Abby Kelley, originally active in the anti-slavery group in Lynn, went to Ohio, lived in a log cabin, lectured widely, and organized the Western Antislavery Society. She later married Stephen Foster, also an abolitionist, and they traveled and lectured together.

The marriage of Angelina Grimké and Theodore Weld was also a union of activists in the antislavery movement. Weld was a powerful preacher who went to Cincinnati and tore apart Lyman Beecher's administration of Lane Theological Seminary, finding the moderation advocated by Beecher inadequate in addressing discrimination against blacks. Weld and his group of students shocked Cincinnati by having picnics and frolics with blacks, and he managed to divert toward Oberlin College in 1835 donations of money which otherwise would have gone to hard-pressed Lane. As Beecher's institution weakened, along with the fortunes of the Stowes and the Beechers, Oberlin prospered. Antoinette Brown and Lucy Stone were students together there.

A list of the guests at the wedding of Weld and Angelina Grimké suggests how broadly based geographically and closely knit emotionally the group was: Lewis Tappan, one of the wealthy Tappan brothers who paid abolitionist legal fees and gave loans and donations to chosen institutions; James Birney, the born-again Southern slave owner; Maria Weston Chapman, the author from Boston; and Abby Kelley.

The most unconventional marriage among the abolitionists was that in 1855 of Lucy Stone to Henry Browne Blackwell of Cincinnati. He was the brother of Dr. Elizabeth Blackwell and of Samuel Blackwell, husband of Antoinette Brown. The couple drew up a "Marriage Protest" against the unfair laws governing married women, and their marriage contract was later published in William Lloyd Garrison's *Liberator* in Boston. Lucy retained her maiden name. They belonged to the conservative wing of the woman suffrage movement, seeking state-by-state endorsement. Together they edited *The Woman's Journal.*

A number of marriages included husband-wife teams. Jane Hitchcock and Benjamin James jointly edited the *Antislavery Bugle*. The husband of Lydia Maria Child, the Boston novelist, was a founder of the New England Antislavery Society. In mid-century, Myra Colby Bradwell studied law under the direction of her husband in Illinois and edited a legal journal. Emma Hart Willard's husband helped her to establish a girls' boarding school; the school she founded in Troy, New York was to become nationally known for the education of women.

However, the arrival of babies, particularly when the family income was small, often provided severe strain for the previously active and ambitious wife. If the pregnancies were accompanied by severe gynecological problems, as was the case with Angelina Grimké Weld, the formerly active woman was reduced to semi-invalidism. Angelina had three children in five years, and her husband, Theodore, was anxious about her health. Her sister Sarah, older by twelve years, remained her live-in companion and assistant to Theodore Weld. The brilliant sisters, whose lectures against slavery had been attended by large audiences and whose writings included the radical argument that because slavery was a sin, a Christian might break the law of a state—these sisters, once retired to domestic life, were little heard from again.

It was a danger that both Theodore Weld and Angelina Grimké had foreseen before their marriage, for they felt their duty as reformers. Weld wrote to Angelina, "We are very prominently identified with the great moral movements of the age. . . . Moral reform, Temperance, Abolition, Rights and sphere of women. . . . Thousands and thousands will watch for your halting. . . . I feel also most solemnly that a peculiar responsibility rests on ME too. . . . "[4]

Weld later felt obliged to curtail his political activism in order to devote more time to his family. Clearly, in the case of the Grimké-Weld relationship, marriage severely limited their work in reforms.

Four Blackwell sisters chose not to marry and instead pursued careers in art, journalism, and medicine; it would seem they believed celibacy necessary for most women who wanted active lives in the world. However, the achievements of Antoinette Brown Blackwell and Elizabeth Cady Stanton show that marriage and a family were not necessarily insurmountable obstacles. However, the requisites were financial security, robust health, mental and physical, and determination almost grim at times. Antoinette Brown Blackwell, who had seven children, remained away from public life for almost twenty years after her marriage.

Not all abolitionist marriage partners remained compatible. Prudence Crandall, a young teacher in Canterbury, Connecticut, had insisted, in spite of community opposition, on opening a boarding school for black female students, and she chose to endure assault, vandalism of her school and her home, arson, ordure dumped in her backyard, two court trials, calumny, and a night in jail. She made what she thought would be a happy marriage when, after her trials, she married a Baptist minister, the Rev. Calvin Philleo, who promised to work with her for the education of blacks. The wedding was in 1834, but many years later, in 1886 in Kansas, she admitted her husband's tyranny. He had not even permitted her to read books of her own choosing![5]

The majority of the suffragists married, but an outstanding woman in the movement, Susan B. Anthony, did not. Elizabeth Stanton often spoke warmly of their friendship and long collaboration. Anthony's father was a Quaker, her mother a Baptist. She taught school, but in 1850 she "hid her ferule away."[6] At a meeting in Seneca Falls, Stanton and Anthony quickly formed a friendship. "In thought and sympathy we were one, and in the division of labor we exactly complemented each other. . . . So entirely one are we that, in all our associations . . . not one feeling of envy or jealousy has ever shadowed our lives."[7]

Suffragists went out of their way to introduce promising recruits to leaders in the movement. For example, Paulina Wright Davis, of Providence, Rhode Island, provided a social occasion so that Isabella Beecher Hooker could talk with Stanton and Anthony.

Not all the suffragists withstood the storms of the struggle. Stanton and Anthony's "New York wing," which was more radical, and the "Boston wing," which was conservative, wasted a considerable amount of energy in infighting. One group promoted the National Woman Suffrage Association, which worked for the ballot by federal amendment, and reforms in divorce, labor, and property laws. The more conservative American Woman Suffrage Association settled for the ballot on a state by state basis. Yet, although some of the quarrels were explosive, at least energy was exchanged; it was probably healthier for women to be engaged in controversy within the suffrage movement than to languish in a water-cure establishment.

The abolitionists too had had controversies within their ranks. The conservatives had advocated Colonization, the gradual freeing of slaves and returning them to Africa, whereas the radicals wanted speedy and total emancipation. It seems likely that in most minority movements, a large number of vocal and impassioned individuals will be difficult to harness in a joint effort. So it was with both abolitionists and suffragists.

A detailed look at the women's rights movement in the nineteenth century shows, as do most reform movements, a search for a constituency, often followed by betrayal by some individuals, then a regrouping and a search for new supporters. The women who worked for woman suffrage showed tremendous persistence and capacity to survive betrayal. Time after time their male allies deserted them in a crisis, and occasionally some of their female allies deserted as well.

The greatest betrayal was for them the perpetuation of male dominance with the words "male citizens" in the 14th Amendment, adopted in 1868. The 13th amendment, adopted in 1865, had abolished slavery and "involuntary servitude." In 1870, when the 15th Amendment was adopted, black men were given the vote. But women, both black and white, many of whom had worked for the abolition of slavery from the 1830's onward, were ignored.

An early leader in the abolitionist movement had been William Lloyd Garrison: the first number of his journal, *The Liberator*, was published in January 1831. However, in 1867 Garrison gave no support at all during the women's campaign in Kansas, at a time when that support was desperately needed. In 1870 in Boston he reversed himself and gave twelve reasons why women should have the vote!

Wendell Phillips, president of the Anti-Slavery Association, was another who disappointed the feminists. In 1866 they invited the Anti-Slavery Association to merge with the women's rights group. It seemed a logical step after so many years of collaboration. But Phillips was able to keep the issue from coming to a vote. Rejected, the women held a women's rights convention in New York City and from it came the American Equal Rights Association.

Another major emotional disappointment that was also a major political setback was the about-face of Horace Greeley, publisher of the leading Republican newspaper, the *New York Tribune*. He had been a strong supporter of the feminist Margaret Fuller, and in 1867 he was active in a movement in New York to abolish the requirement of $250 as a property qualification before a black man could vote. Greeley and his cohorts used the support of women to defeat this antiblack requirement, but then abandoned the same women when the time came to declare for female suffrage.

New York and Kansas were the two arenas after the Civil War that saw the most intense struggle for woman suffrage, and the most bitter defeats. Kansas, which had a history of a vigorous abolitionist movement, seemed a hospitable place for a campaign for woman suffrage. Provision for a referendum on the vote for women had been introduced in the legislature by a rebel Republican faction. Lucy Stone and her husband, Henry Blackwell, left the East for Kansas and did three months of intensive campaigning. Later Elizabeth Stanton and Susan Anthony joined in the campaign and found among the tired farm women the disillusion that followed hard work on land that was not as fertile as their men had fantasied. Rather the fields were often marginal acres with minimal return.

The campaign by the reformers, which lasted nine months, received no help from the editors of three antislavery journals who might have made a difference. They were Greeley, Phillips, editor of the *National Antislavery Standard*, and Theodore Tilton, editor of the *Independent*, who was to be a principal figure in the allegations of adultery against Henry Ward Beecher. Indeed, the scandal that developed around Beecher, who was generally a friend of the women's movement, was to give gratification to many enemies of the movement. The scandal served as an attack not only upon Beecher himself, but also upon the alleged immoral ideas of the women's movement, such as criticism of the married state, and the endorsement by Victoria Woodhull of sexual freedom for women as well as men.

Since the majority of the Republican party were more willing to woo the new black male voters than to support the vote for women, Susan Anthony and Elizabeth Stanton accepted an offer of support in Kansas from a wealthy and eccentric financier and railroad speculator, George Train. But Train was also known as a racist, and his support caused criticism within the Equal Rights Party from which the group never recovered. Susan Anthony came under particular attack.

The only healthy result of the campaign in Kansas in 1867 was the founding, financed by George Train, according to Stanton, of the *Revolution*, a daring feminist periodical.[8] In its pages were articles about "female farmers, inventors, sailors, and thieves . . . " along with information about sex education and the controversial communities of the Mormons and Perfectionists.[9]

Unfortunately, the "help" of woman suffragists became associated with lost elections. Woman suffragists supported Salmon Chase as a presidential candidate, but by June of 1868 Chase's campaign collapsed from lack of support in the Democratic party. In some constituencies, endorsement by the Equal Rights Association meant a kiss of death. In addition, active women reformers were so small in number that they were not taken seriously by the parties at the national level.

A new group of feminist adherents came with the founding of the Working Women's Association in 1868, in which Susan Anthony and the *Revolution* were key factors. Most women workers were not organized: seventy per cent of women who worked were domestics, and about twenty-four per cent were in the textile, clothing, and shoe industries. The most skilled woman workers were the typesetters, and these joined forces with the suffragists, although the association lasted only a year.

The most encouraging support for women from the labor movement came with the formation of the National Labor Union in 1866. The union was composed largely of white skilled male workers with a trades union background. They were willing to support women and blacks, but a speech by leader William Sylvis emphasized the nurturing role, not the working role, of women. Athough he believed women workers were entitled to the same wages and working hours as men and to any improvement effected in working conditions, he declared also that "woman . . . was created to be the presiding deity of the home circle, the instructor of our children."[10] His National Labor Union lasted for only six years, but it represented a slight leavening in the attitude of men unionists toward women workers.

Women were also active in the Farmers' Alliance, which later became the Populist party, but only one woman held national office in the organization. Traditionally, women throughout the nineteenth century had attended political rallies, prepared the food for them, and sometimes participated actively in work for improvement in working conditions. Massachusetts mill workers, for example, most of them women, had been active even early in the century in petitioning the state to improve working conditions.

In view of the participation of many women in reform activities outside the home, there remains to be discussed the major question of why the vote for women took so long to achieve. For no reform in the United States was longer aborning than suffrage for women. It took some thirty years for the manifestos against slavery to produce the Emancipation Proclamation of 1863, and the Fifteenth Amendment. But it took seventy-two years, from 1848 until 1920, to produce adoption of the Nineteenth Amendment. The words were: "The right of citizens of the United States to vote shall not be denied or abridged by the United States or by any State on account of sex."

12

MINORITIES WITHIN A MINORITY

Elizabeth Cady Stanton and Susan B. Anthony can scarcely be said to represent all of American women, but their reform minority was large compared with the tiny minority, composed of both men and women, who established some five hundred independent communities in the United States in the nineteenth century. These communities, according to a study by Raymond Lee Muncy can be divided into three kinds: sectarian, which looked to eternal life as well as earthly life; reform, which sought to improve the social and economic conditions of nineteenth-century capitalism; and economic, which broke down differences between capital and labor.[1] In practice, the distinctions were often blurred. All the communities were alike in that they isolated themselves from conventional settlements. Most members felt that blood and legal ties were neither the most important nor the most virtuous ties for binding people together; and most members lived in ways that the outside world regarded as extremely unconventional, and even wicked.

Most leaders of the communities were charismatic and authoritarian. "Mother" Ann Lee, who emigrated from Liverpool with some of her followers in 1774, was probably the most grandiose of any leader in her conception of her role: she considered herself the female nature of Jesus Christ. Without systematic managers, however, her followers might have dispersed. James Whitaker and Joseph Meacham, who founded the first Shaker Village, at Watervliet, New York, in 1787, deserve credit for the expansion of the Shaker group.

The Shakers, in their preparation for the Resurrection, declared against sexual intercourse and for celibacy. Married couples who joined the group had to agree to give up sexual relations. The position of women was based on parity between the sexes, except that men were more likely to do heavy outdoor work, and women indoor work. However, both sexes were eligible to become Elders. Shaker settlements lasted more than a hundred and fifty years and are regarded by some as a variation on nunneries and monasteries, although clearly the analogy is not a close one.

The writings of François Fourier, as published in 1822, offer the most comprehensive, and occasionally bizarre, thinking about utopian communities that has ever been printed. Fourier, the son of a well-to-do family, tried to avoid the career as a businessman that his father had programmed for him, but from his work in Lyons in his youth, learning how the silk workers lived and labored, to his adventurous days as a traveling salesman, he remained fascinated by "bourgeois fraud and mercantile hypocrisy." He developed an elaborate theory which was the foundation for many small self-sustaining cooperative communities in the United States.

Fourier's hypothesis was that man is considerably more virtuous than society is, and that his potential for virtue can be developed in a special environment, in a "phalanx," which is to be a practical facsimile of the ideal realm of Harmony. Through the principle of "passionate attraction," men and women will work together in harmony, without exploitation.

Fourier was not very successful in finding backers in France for such communities. The construction by Fourierist workers of a pig pen with walls eighteen inches thick and with no entrance made it clear that workers needed skills as well as good intentions![2] However, Fourier benefited from the split in the Saint-Simon adherents, and many of the former supporters of Saint-Simon joined the Fourier circle. Albert Brisbane was born in New York state and studied under Fourier in France. He was a major publicist in the United States of Fourier's ideas. For Horace Greeley's *New York Tribune* he wrote columns on

Fourierism. With Greeley's backing, Margaret Fuller was also able to publish her *Woman in the Nineteenth Century*, in 1845. Fuller was an advocate of Fourier's pronouncements, the most radical of which for women was his opinion on love and duty.

> The moralists are . . . ridiculous in their opinions about love; they wish love to be ruled by constancy and fidelity, which are so incompatible with the designs of nature and so wearisome to both sexes that no creature remains constant when he enjoys complete liberty.[3]

Certainly Fourier's belief that bourgeois society had created sexual fraud was one endorsed not only by radicals like Victoria Woodhull but by moderate feminists such as Elizabeth Stanton.

Another male leader, charismatic in personality, was John Humphrey Noyes. Born in Vermont, educated at Dartmouth and in theology at Andover and Yale, he knew about Fourier and about the practical experiment of Brook Farm in Massachusetts, a haven for intellectual men and women willing to do farm labor together.

Noyes, like Fourier, disagreed with the Calvinist view of the natural depravity of man. His doctrine of Perfectionism began with a Bible school in Putney, Vermont, and grew gradually into a community of friends, and, later, of shared property and affection. The group was small; in 1843 there were only thirty-five converts. Noyes at first advocated celibacy, and held the theory of "spiritual affinity," the theory that close harmony between men and women can exist without the carnal. The female sex was for Noyes part of the godhead, since God was both male and female.

Noyes decided later that celibacy would lead to the end of the community, since, as with the Shakers, children would have to be adopted, not begotten. He did not view monogamy, however, as consistent with his Perfectionist beliefs, and so he developed the idea of "complex marriage," which permitted intercourse with varied partners, but which avoided promiscuity by making Noyes the ultimate arbiter of sexual activity within the group. In addition, as with the Shakers' Elders, senior members of the group sanctioned by Noyes acted as intermediaries and counselors.

In spite of these limitations, the townspeople of Putney, many of them, regarded Noyes and his group as dangerous and immoral. In 1848 the group moved to Oneida, New York, where they were eighty-seven in number. Noyes remained the patriarch and developed a theory, which became eagerly accepted, of sexual activity based on male self-control. Coitus with a variety of partners was encouraged because Noyes believed that use of the sexual organs was not evil unless exclusive sexual right in another person was assumed; or unless the sexual act led to procreation. Noyes' own wife had had four stillbirths, and he argued that intercourse with ejaculation produced unwanted pregnancies, and that coitus interruptus, the dominant form of Victorian birth control, produced a spent, exhausted male and an anxious woman. Instead, intercourse without ejaculation was encouraged and taught as a technique.

When children were conceived, it was usually with the approval of the group after careful consideration. Stirpiculture it was called by Noyes, scientific breeding with the consent of the breeders. Occasionally pregnancies occurred without such careful consideration, but these were exceptions to the rule.

Even the so-called maternal instinct was contested by Noyes, and the child too was taught that he could not have his mother's attention on demand. "If a child called to its mother from a window in the children's house, the mother was forbidden to acknowledge its plea."[4]

The Oneida community lasted until almost the end of the nineteenth century, but gradually monogamous marriage recurred, as did the holding of private property. The Oneida precepts had lasted about thirty-five years.

The Harmonists, or Rappites, thrived for almost a century. They, like the Shakers, advocated celibacy, but did not enforce it. The Rapps, Frederick and George, who were German Pietists, held absolute authority over the German farmers, and their interpretations of the word of the Bible, including the Second Coming of Christ, were accepted. In practical terms the communities did well—in Harmony, Pennsylvania, then in Harmony, Indiana, and in Economy, Pennsylvania. Robert Dale Owen, whose father purchased the former Rapp community in Harmony, Indiana, declared that the success of the community had come from "unquestioning submission to an autocrat."[5] Economic success they had indeed: their original wealth was twenty-five dollars a person; by 1825 it was two thousand dollars a person.

Few of the leaders in the utopian communities embroiled themselves in the politics of the majority. Robert Dale Owen was one of the few. The Owenites believed in the equality of women and permitted divorce when both partners expressed what today would be called "irreconcilable differences." Owen spoke impressively at the Indiana Constitutional Convention in 1850, not in behalf of the vote for women, which, he thought, they had no chance of achieving, but in behalf of a woman's right to own and control property, whether the property was acquired before or after her marriage. The principle was made law in Indiana.

Very different from the freedom of woman in the Owenite community was the inferior status given her by the Mormons, the Church of Jesus Christ of Latter-Day Saints. According to the United Order of Enoch, all property belongs to the Church and individual Mormons are its custodians. However, the polygamy advocated at first by Joseph Smith, and then by his successor, Brigham Young, made women subject to autocratic husbands. One of the crudest remarks about wives uttered in the nineteenth century came from Mormon John Doyle Lee, who had sixteen to eighteen wives and sixty-four children. (He was executed in 1877 after a second trial which found him guilty of leading a murderous attack against a group of emigrants to California.)

> I could have perfect Hell with my wives were I to listen to them, but when ever [sic] one begans [sic] to strut & lead out, I say go it & show your wisdom & soon she gets ashamed & curls down.[6]

In testimony before Congress soon after the end of the nineteenth century, prominent men in the Mormon church declared that polygamy was no longer endorsed. However, as recently as 1979, support of the Equal Rights Amendment by a woman Mormon led to her being censured by the church. And back in 1856 there was almost a rebellion of Mormon wives until Brigham Young told them firmly from the pulpit that they had two weeks to conform or else to leave the church.

They conformed. The patriarchal system was even more firmly entrenched in the Mormon church than in the churches of the Protestant majority.

13

CONTRASTS—AN OVERVIEW

Siblings are good subjects for comparison because they share not only some of the same genetic material but usually a similar social environment. Three of the Beecher sisters, Catharine, Harriet, and Isabella (Isabella was their half-sister), show considerable variety in their dealing with important conflicts.

Catharine, the eldest, was a substitute mother for Harriet and the other children of her father's first marriage, and she remained the dominant child when her father remarried. She founded a successful school for girls in the East, a less successful one in the Middle West, and commandeered the services of her younger sisters as teaching assistants.

She was ambitious but also eager to please her father, who was domineering but often affectionate and jovial. Catharine was saddened to see all her brothers sent on to higher education while she remained at home. She rationalized her disappointment, however. Self-taught, she knew *more*, she declared, than her brothers did.

For some years she maintained a high place in the pecking order of the family, at least among her sisters. When Harriet married a poor teacher and had several children within a few years, Catharine seemed the relatively secure sister, writing and earning a living. It even appeared, when Harriet remained in a sanatarium for almost a year, that Harriet might be a victim of chronic depression. But Harriet returned to her family, and despite incapacitating headaches and moods of depression, she continued to write and, in 1852, produced the astonishingly successful *Uncle Tom's Cabin*. After this triumph, she was taken seriously for most of the years of her long life.

As Harriet's star rose, Catharine's faded. Her second school, the one in Cincinnati, did not do well, and the success of her book on household management, which had Harriet's name as coauthor, must have left her with a small fear that she was riding on her sister's coattails. Furthermore, even though she tried to dignify household management, the subject was scarcely the intellectual challenge she once had responded to when writing about religion. It can be argued that Catharine's determined effort to make household management an important matter was also an attempt to have herself taken seriously.

Certainly she had friends and many acquaintances. Her survey in 1855 "of female health" was dependent upon data furnished her by scores of acquaintances in many cities. But most of these women had given up. Most of them considered themselves invalids or semi-invalids.

Catharine continued to believe that in politics it was enough to ask in order to receive. She wrote, "Why should we not . . . *ask for the things needed*, instead of the circuitous and uncertain mode involved in the ballot?"[1] She seemed to ignore the fact that since 1848 Elizabeth Cady Stanton, Lucretia Mott, and others had been "asking" for suffrage and other reforms— with little success. Catharine was distressed by what she called "all the antagonisms that are warring on the family state. Spiritualism, free-love, free divorce . . . the worldliness which tempts men and women to avoid *large* families. . . . "[2] She seemed not to remember the violent headaches and bouts of temporary blindness that had overtaken her sister during and after her frequent pregnancies.

Harriet was amenable to the vote for women, as expressed in "Servants," an 1864 article published in *The Atlantic Monthly*, but usually she wrote with nostalgia about the allegedly noble days when Puritan women tended garden and dairy, span, and raised large numbers of children. Yet, in another mood, she described the real-life, hardworking nursemaid-companion in the early Beecher household, Esther, as an exhausted woman who had no private life whatever; it was often difficult for Harriet to distinguish between fantasy and reality. During her years of successful writing, her headaches and blindness disappeared and she became increasingly conservative, looking back to an allegedly better American past.

Isabella, never as well-known as either Catharine or Harriet, was also required by her father to support herself at an early age and to go without an advanced education while her brothers pursued theirs. She married a young attorney, reared children, and in 1869 sought a niche in the woman's movement, at first in Connecticut, and later in the national suffrage organization. In the 1850's and early 1860's, however, she experienced severe depression.

It took courage for middle-aged and middle-class women, raised to conform and to be gentle and passive, to come out of the parlors and speak in hired halls. A few had had practice with speeches on temperance. Newspaper reporters were smitten with the novelty: one reporter described a woman from Boston as "a lady in middle life with a winning, refined face . . . unaccustomed to speak in rooms larger than a parlor. . . ."[3]

Many sheltered middle-class "ladies" were indeed nervous. More self-confident women like Margaret Fuller Ossoli, Elizabeth Cady Stanton, Susan B. Anthony, young republican orator Anna Dickinson, and Victoria Woodhull had no difficulty on the lecture platform. Fuller and Anthony had been teachers, and Stanton and Woodhull had long experience in leading meetings. Anthony had been involved in temperance work, Stanton in the antislavery movement; they had served their apprenticeships before launching into the woman's suffrage movement.

To be successful, it was certainly an asset to be middle class, comfortable if not rich, relatively well-educated, and provided within one's family (usually by father) with models for assertiveness. These advantages were held by Stanton and Anthony. This is not to say, however, that they received constant encouragement from the key people in their lives. At the age of forty, Elizabeth wrote to Susan in 1855: "I wish that I were as free as you and I would stump the state in a twinkling. But I am not, and what is more, I passed through a terrible

scourging when last at my father's. . . . I never felt more
keenly the degradation of my sex. . . . Henry sides with my
friends, who oppose me in all that is dearest to my heart."[4]

The friendship of the two women sustained them through
such criticism and through the trials of many years, from
stumping in Kansas to abuse in lecture halls. Stanton was the
rhetorician, Anthony the organizer, and each respected the
other and felt fondness as well. In spite of the schism in the
woman's movement, the two remained friends.

Their middle-class background did not make them scorn
women lacking their credentials. Stanton especially believed
that the woman's movement should include a broad spectrum.
Hence, in a fervent letter to Lucretia Mott, she defended the
radical Victoria Woodhull. Woodhull often dressed in a bizarre way, was said to have lovers and to be a bigamist. In
some quarters, she was considered an embarrassment to the
woman's movement. Her principal achievement in the United
States (she later migrated to England, married, and edited
The Humanitarian) was to lay bare hypocrisy in American life,
often using *Woodhull and Claflin's Weekly* as her medium. She
was incensed at the double standard that was prevalent in
public morality. Her rage against the Reverend Henry Ward
Beecher was caused principally by his and his partisans' attempts to cover up his adulterous affair with one of his pa-
rishioners.

She was a worrisome ally in the women's movement, as Anthony came to believe, because of her desire to form a people's
party in 1872. But in a letter of 1872, Stanton wrote in defense of Woodhull: "This woman stands before us today as an
able speaker and writer. . . . We have already women enough
sacrificed to this sentimental, hypocritical prating about purity, without going out of our way to increase the number. . . . If this present woman must be crucified, let men
drive the spikes."[5] Such a defense of a maverick woman was
relatively rare.

Historically, serious friendship between women has not been
regarded highly, at least by men. Montaigne declared in his
essay "Of Friendship": "The ordinary capacity of women is inadequate for the communion and fellowship which is the nurse

of this sacred bond; nor does their soul seem firm enough to endure the strain. . . . [6]

One of the most important effects of the woman's movement in the nineteenth century was that it fostered a bonding that went beyond the family and the friendships of adolescence. Nor was it the temporary bonding that occurs between women in such key events as the birthing of a child, when a neighbor or midwife becomes an important temporary helper but may not be incorporated into a desire for a long-term relationship.

There can be bonding between victims, of course, and this is possibly what happened to Catharine Beecher when she joined the ranks of the water-cure visitors. By contrast, Stanton and Anthony turned their anger against "the system" and chose assertive, creative activity. They were financially more fortunate than many women, but their relatively comfortable circumstances did not lead them to indolence. Both their resentment against male power and their sympathy for others of their sex caused them to speak for the large number of their less verbal and aggressive sisters. Aggressiveness was needed particularly by minority women: Sojourner Truth went so far as to bare her breasts at a public meeting, after she was accused of being a man masquerading as a woman. [7]

Of the several women who could be chosen as exemplars among nineteenth-century American women, Margaret Fuller and Elizabeth Cady Stanton are among the most impressive—one whose accomplishments occurred early in the century, the other renowned later in the century.

Fuller actually was only five years younger than Stanton, but she is placed in the early decades, since her relatively short life ended in shipwreck and drowning with her small family in 1850. The end of Fuller's life lies close to the beginning of Stanton's work for women's rights, work that did not end until the end of Stanton's long life, in 1902. Stanton outlived the precocious but ill-fated Fuller by more than half a century.

Fuller's life, although short, was filled with cosmopolitan and international interests. A precocious child, dominated by a father whose intellectual demands upon her were severe, she became a young woman of immense learning and a friend of brilliant men in the Cambridge establishment. Because of the sudden death of her father, she was forced to earn a living as a teacher. Later she led "Conversations" among prestigious Boston women that were rather more Socratic in intent than the usual Lyceum-like lectures.

At the age of thirty, she became editor of the newly established *Dial*, the Transcendental quarterly. A contributor also of essays, she expanded their content into a book, *Woman in the Nineteenth Century*. A subsequent trip to the West provided her with material for another book, and this in turn led Horace Greeley of the New York *Tribune* to offer her a job.

For Greeley's newspaper, Fuller wrote on assorted subjects, including the hardships of immigrants bursting into the ports of entry. Perhaps these perceptions, Alice Rossi speculates, led to the "radical sympathies" that Fuller formed when she went to Europe in 1846.[8] In London she met Mazzini, the Italian nationalist and liberator, and in Italy she met and married Angelo Ossoli, also a Republican, although born to a family of the aristocracy.

Fuller's writings about women include an analogy to slaves— an analogy often in the minds of women activists. She declared, "In slavery, acknowledged slavery, women are on a par with men. Each is a work-tool, an article of property—no more!"[9]

The typical marriage, she believed, was a form of enslavement for the woman. "That is the very fault of marriage and of the present relation between the sexes, that the woman does belong to the man, instead of forming a whole with him. . . . It is a vulgar error that love, *a* love to woman is her whole existence."[10]

Margaret Fuller's early death put an end to any hope she might have had for a new kind of family and career in the United States. But Elizabeth Cady Stanton was fortunate in living a long life during which she was able to work out the feelings and thoughts of her earlier years. Her childhood, as we have seen, was dominated by a desire to excel, to shine in her father's eyes as a worthy substitute for his only son who died as a youth.

Elizabeth Cady married Henry Stanton, a lawyer and politician, and later a journalist. They remained married for forty-six years. Like her father, he was sympathetic to the antislavery and temperance movements, but also like her father, he was uncomfortable with the women's rights movement and Elizabeth's public lectures on the subject. (Elizabeth's father actually disinherited her when she chose to lecture publicly on women's rights, although later he reinstated her in his will.)

Elizabeth Stanton was no paragon, and she had strong variations in mood. She bore seven children; she was proud of them all, and of her quick recovery after each birth. Yet she wrote to Susan Anthony when she was thirty-seven, "How much do I long to be free from housekeeping and children, so as to have some time to read, and think, and write. But it may be well for me to understand all the trials of woman's lot, that I may more eloquently proclaim them when the time comes."[11]

It is accurate to say that she was glad she had children, and it is also accurate to say that she recognized the restrictions they placed on her life. With honesty and generosity, she eulogized in writing the loyal housekeeper who had helped make possible for her the care of a family as well as the mission of reform.[12]

Elizabeth Stanton made enemies. She had a sharp tongue. Furthermore, her endorsement of the radical feminist Victoria Woodhull alienated many conservative members of the women's movement. Not until 1890 was the rift healed, when the two rival organizations combined as the National American Woman Suffrage Association.

This schism should not be viewed lightly. Newspapers recorded the bitter infighting. At the Equal Rights Convention in New York City in May 1869, an angry note was sounded by Stephen Foster, husband of activist Abby Kelley, when he criticized the auditing of finances. He implied strongly that Susan Anthony had been cavalier in her expenses and reimbursements. (The budget for the previous year was listed as $1,745.97 "receipts and expenditures.")

The same issue of *The Hartford Daily Courant*, May 14, 1869, recorded "a lively little set to" at that meeting between Susan Anthony and Frederick Douglass, the distinguished black antislavery leader. Douglass expressed his gratitude to Elizabeth Stanton for the "refuge" she had given him, but he criticized her speaking of "Sambo" as preferred to "the daughter of Washington and Jefferson." He insisted that the plight of black people was far more painful than that of white women. Apparently Anthony defended Stanton during the exchange.

In 1895, when Stanton's first volume of *The Woman's Bible* was published, she offended still more people. However, even as early as 1881, the published preface to Volume One of *The History of Woman Suffrage* shows that Stanton and her coauthors considered the church to be hostile to the woman suffrage movement.

Stanton described herself as often "at a boiling point," but her close friendship with Susan Anthony enabled her to express her anger, and indeed she believed that such expression was therapeutic.[13] "I think if women were to indulge more freely in vituperation, they would enjoy ten times the health they do. It seems to me they are suffering from repression."[14]

All the feminists expressed a sense of legitimate anger at the restrictions under which women were placed. Clearly the Victorian myth of woman's sphere was a myth they believed imprisoned them.

14

MYTH AND STRUGGLE

The dominant patriarchal myth about the American Victorian woman was that "woman's sphere" was separate from, but equal to—possibly superior to—the sphere of the male. However, the women who wrote the early volumes of the *History of Woman Suffrage*, Elizabeth Cady Stanton, Susan B. Anthony, and Matilda Joslyn Gage, published in 1881 in the preface to the second volume a stinging analysis of the opposition.

> The narrow self-interest of all classes is opposed to the sovereignty of woman. The rulers in the State are not willing to share their power with a class equal if not superior to themselves, over which they could never hope for absolute control. . . . The annointed leaders in the Church are equally hostile to freedom for a sex supposed for wise purposes to have been subordinated by divine decree. . . . Of the autocrat in the home, John Stuart Mill has well said, "No ordinary man is willing to find at his own fireside an equal in the person he calls wife."[1]

This declaration in both content and style contrasts strongly with passages reprinted even after her death in 1865, from Lydia Sigourney, popular poet and essayist. In *Whisper to a Bride* she wrote, "Trusting One, whither wilt thou follow thy beloved? From the nest where thou wert reared? from the hearth-stone where thy first affections grew?—to take thy place at his board, and to beautify a new home with the love that never dies?"[2]

Unlike Lydia Sigourney, the women reformers did not want to feel vulnerable, did not want to be "Trusting Ones." Yet married middle-class women were often tempted to stay out of the fray and remain at home with the family. Elizabeth Stanton gave credit to her friend Susan Anthony for encouragement in "missionary labors." "With the cares of a large family, I might, in time, like so many women, have become wholly absorbed in a narrow family selfishness. . . . "[3]

"Narrow family selfishness"—daring words, when contrasted with those of Catharine Beecher, "Woman . . . is the chief minister of the family estate in the Christian family."[4] Beecher sought conscientiously to elevate household management into a dignified and worthy occupation, suitable for that "chief minister of the family estate," and indeed even Stanton respected her own manifold duties at home while her children were young; but Stanton believed family interests to be too narrow and limited.

However, the fact remains that a very large number of women worked outside the home in order to survive—ten to twelve hours a day, up to six days a week, in factory, field, or in tenements doing "piece work." Such women had little opportunity to work for women's rights, and little encouragement.

Rich, poor, or middle-class, all women had in common, as Stanton said in her reminiscences, that they "ranked with idiots, lunatics, and criminals in the Constitution, the negro has been the only respectable compeer we had. . . . "[5] Nevertheless, the majority of women in any class did not work for woman suffrage. Even among middle-class women reformers there was no unanimity on the subject. Frances Willard, a leader in the Woman's Christian Temperance Union, had to struggle for many years within the Union to gather support from conservatives for the vote for women.[6] Most women workers in factories were uninterested in the middle-class suffragists, who seldom extended their efforts into specific improvements in working conditions. In any case, most women factory workers were insecure people, disliked and rejected by most male factory workers for their roles as strikebreakers and cut-rate employees.

The lack of a clear-cut constituency is a practical reason for the long delay in the vote for women. Both men and women had labored as abolitionists, but only a small number of either sex felt indignation over the deprivation of the ballot for women. Why the lack of a clear-cut constituency? As late as 1920, when women received the vote by amendment to the Constitution, a few Southern political figures believed that the vote for black women would cause an unwanted surge in black power at the polls, but this racist basis for opposition to the vote for women does not contradict the larger fear that the American family would be undermined.

It was not a case of males wanting women to stay out of politics—so long as women did not sit in legislatures or vote against issues favored by men! Women for decades had provided the food and swelled the crowds at political rallies throughout the nation. They had demonstrated before saloons in order to close them down, and early in the nineteenth century women mill workers in Massachusetts had petitioned the Commonwealth for improved working conditions. However, a petition is not the same as a demand. The entire psychological set is different.

From the emancipation of women, men feared, as did conservative women, that a new household would emerge. The old reformers, like Stanton (1815–1902), as well as the newer ones, like Charlotte Perkins Gilman (1860–1935), recognized that they would face hostility and ridicule. Gilman speculated about the changes that would be required in institutions. In 1898 in *Women and Economics*, she discussed the need for such new arrangements as "a commodious and well-served apartment house for professional women with families. . . . The apartments would be without kitchens; but there would be a kitchen belonging to the house."[7]

Like Stanton, Gilman believed that female emancipation, including economic independence, "necessarily involves a change in the home and family relation." She continued,

If that change is for the advantage of individual and race, we need not fear it. It does not involve a change in the marriage relation except in withdrawing the element of economic dependence, nor in the relation of mother to child save to improve it. But it does involve the exercise of human faculty in women, in social service and exchange rather than in domestic service solely.[8]

Gilman, but not the majority, believed that the family would benefit from a new order. "The more absolutely woman is segregated to sex-functions only, cut off from all economic use, and made wholly dependent on the sex-relation as means of livelihood, the more pathological does her motherhood become."[9]

On the other hand, Catharine Beecher, also an intelligent and compassionate woman, stood for perpetuation of the myth of woman in control of destiny. Her warm dedication in *The American Woman's Home*, 1869, was to "The Women of America, in whose hands rest the real destinies of the republic." Charged with moral and practical duties in rearing the young, "the Christian family" was also obligated to help the less fortunate. It was with indignation almost biblical that Beecher contrasted, in the same volume, the deprivation and disease endured by the poor in New York City with the "millions of wealth placed in the hands of men and women who profess to be followers of Jesus Christ."

What she yearned for was no less than a spiritual revival in America, led by noble women, and resulting in heightened conscience and compassion in all Americans. For her such an ideal went far beyond the secular goal of woman suffrage. Yet the suffragists were compassionate people too. The many women to whom the authors of the *History of Woman Suffrage* dedicated their first volume in 1881 were hailed "affectionately" as leading, or having led, "Earnest Lives." Mary Wollstonecraft's name was placed in first position.

These women were praised both for their "Earnest Lives," and for their "Fearless Words," for choosing to act upon their belief in equal rights for equal beings under law—a new political and social equality that would sweep away the myths.

NOTES

The individuals to whom the authors of the *History of Woman Suffrage*—Elizabeth Cady Stanton, Susan B. Anthony, and Matilda Joslyn Gage—"affectionately inscribed" Volume One in 1881 are: Frances Wright, Lucretia Mott, Harriet Martineau, Lydia Marie Child, Margaret Fuller, Sarah and Angelina Grimké, Josephine S. Griffing, Martha C. Wright, Harriot K. Hunt, M.D., Lydia Mott, Elizabeth W. Farnham, Lydia F. Fowler, M.D., Paulina Wright Davis.

Mary Wollstonecraft's name is listed first and separately.

Reporters and the public seemed obsessed with the image of women wearing "trowsers." In one week alone of May, May 7–14 of 1869, the *Hartford Daily Courant* printed in small headlines "A Woman Doctor in Trowsers in the White House"; Mrs. Stanton's advocacy of "bifurcated garments"; and the description of a woman delegate to the Equal Rights Convention in New York City as a being "who, if she wore breeches, nobody would mistake for a woman."

Chapter 1

1. Gerda Lerner, ed., *Black Women in White America* (New York: Random House/Vintage, 1973), pp. xvii, xxii.

2. Carl N. Degler, *At Odds: Women and the Family in America from the Revolution to the Present* (New York: Oxford University Press, 1980), p. 308.

3. Helen L. Sumner, *History of Women in Industry in the United States* (New York: Arno Press, 1974), p. 27, from 1910 U.S. Bureau of Labor Statistics.

4. Philip S. Foner, ed., *Mother Jones Speaks* (New York: Monad Press, 1983), p. 5, from testimony of Mother Jones before the House Committee on Rules, Washington, D.C., June 14, 1910.

5. Degler, *At Odds*, p. 155.

6. Catharine E. Beecher, *Woman Suffrage and Woman's Profession* (Hartford, Conn.: Brown and Gross, 1871), p. 33.

7. Degler, *At Odds*, p. 325.

8. Catharine E. Beecher and Harriet Beecher Stowe, *The American Woman's Home* (New York: J. B. Ford, 1869), p. i. See also p. 19.

9. Jacob A. Riis, *How the Other Half Lives*, ed. S. B. Warner, Jr. (Cambridge, Mass.: The Belknap Press of Harvard University Press, 1970), p. 171.

10. Degler, *At Odds*, p. 308.

11. Catharine E. Beecher, *Letters to the People on Health and Happiness* (New York: Harper, 1855), reprinted in Nancy F. Cott, ed., *Root of Bitterness* (New York: E. P. Dutton, 1972), p. 264, and in Gail Parker, ed., *The Oven Birds* (New York, Doubleday/Anchor, 1972), p. 173.

12. Peter Gay, *The Bourgeois Experience*, Vol. I (New York: Oxford University Press, 1984), p. 136.

13. Gay, *The Bourgeois Experience*, from the Diaries of Mabel Loomis Todd, pp. 461–462.

14. Degler, *At Odds*, p. 22. See also Gay, *Bourgeois Experience*, p. 129.

15. Degler, *At Odds*, pp. 168–169.

16. *The Hartford Times*, May 15, 1869.

17. Jeffrey L. Geller, M.D., "Women's Accounts of Psychiatric Illness and Institutionalization," *Hospital and Community Psychiatry* 36 (October 1985): 1057.

18. Julie Roy Jeffrey, *Frontier Women* (New York: Hill and Wang, 1979), p. 14.

19. Ibid., p. 19.

20. Elizabeth F. Baker, *Technology and Women's Work* (New York: Columbia University Press, 1964), pp. 75–77.

Chapter 2

1. S. V. Hale, ed., "Happiness or Ruth Brook," *Juvenile Miscellany* 2 (June 1835).

2. Ibid., p. 165.

3. S. V. Hale, ed., "Lucy and Her Monkey," *Juvenile Miscellany* 2 (June 1835).

4. Ibid, p. 180.

5. Anne Farnam, "Woman Suffrage as an Alternative to the Beecher Ministry," in *Portraits of a Nineteenth Century Family*, ed. Earl A. French and Diana Royce, (Hartford, Conn.: Stowe-Day Foundation, 1976), p. 77.

6. S. V. Hale, ed., "An Agreeable Surprise," *Juvenile Miscellany* 2 (June 1835).

7. S. V. Hale, ed., "Dear William," *Juvenile Miscellany* 2 (June 1835).

8. *The Well Bred Boy* (Boston: William Crosby, 1839).

9. *The Sunday School Teacher's Funeral*, advertisement in *Juvenile Miscellany* 2 (June 1835): 216.

10. John Piermont, ed., *Exercises in Reading and Recitation* (Boston: Charles Bowen, 1836), p. 84.

11. Heinrich Hoffmann, M.D., *Struwwelpeter* (Great Britain: Blackie, 1845).

12. Ibid.

13. William J. Baker, ed., *America Perceived: A View from Abroad in the 19th Century* (West Haven, Conn.: Pendulum Press, 1974), pp. 26–27.

14. Stephen Crane, *Maggie* (n.p., 1893).

15. Mark Twain, *Adventures of Huckleberry Finn*, ed. Henry N. Smith (Boston: Houghton Mifflin, 1958), chapter 6.

16. Ibid., chapter 18.

17. Herman Melville, *Moby-Dick* (London: Collier-Macmillan, 1969), chapter 94.

18. Margaret Fuller Ossoli, *Woman in the Nineteenth Century*, ed. Arthur B. Fuller (Boston: Roberts Brothers, 1874; Westport, Conn.: Greenwood Press, 1968, 1974), with an introduction by Horace Greeley.

Chapter 3

1. Martha Finley, *Elsie's Girlhood* (New York: Dodd Mead, 1872).

2. Gerda Lerner, ed., *Black Women in White America* (New York: Random House/Vintage, 1973), pp. 42–45.

3. Dickinson to Mrs. J. G. Holland, 20 January 1856, in *The Letters of Emily Dickinson*, Vol. II, ed. Thomas H. Johnson (Cambridge, Mass.: Belknap Press, 1958), no. 324.

4. Dickinson to Mrs. Joseph Haven, early summer 1858, in *Letters*, II, ed. Johnson, no. 191.

5. Emily Dickinson, "I Cannot Live with You," in *The Poems of Emily Dickinson*, Vol. II, ed. Thomas H. Johnson (Cambridge, Mass.: Belknap Press, 1958), no. 640.

6. Dickinson to Louise and Frances Norcross, mid-October 1863, in *Letters*, II, ed. Johnson, no. 286.

7. Dickinson to Mrs. J. G. Holland, mid-December 1882, in *The Letters of Emily Dickinson*, Vol. III, ed. Thomas H. Johnson (Cambridge, Mass.: Belknap Press, 1958), no. 792.

8. Dickinson to Louise and Frances Norcross, late November 1882, in *Letters*, III, ed. Johnson, no. 785.

9. Dickinson to Mrs. J. Howard Sweetser, November 1882, in *Letters*, III, ed. Johnson, no. 782.

10. Dickinson to Otis P. Lord, 3 December 1882, in *Letters*, III, ed. Johnson, no. 790.

11. Carroll Smith-Rosenberg, "The Female Word of Love and Ritual: Relations between Women in Nineteenth-Century America," *Signs: Journal of Women in Culture and Society* 1 (Autumn 1975): 17.

12. Dickinson to Jane Humphrey, 12 May 1842, in *The Letters of Emily Dickinson*, Vol. I, ed. Thomas H. Johnson (Cambridge, Mass.: Belknap Press, 1958), no. 3.

13. Dickinson to Jane Humphrey, 3 April 1850, in *Letters*, I, ed. Johnson, no. 35.

14. Dickinson to Jane Humphrey, April 1852, in *Letters*, I, ed. Johnson, no. 86.

15. Dickinson to Jane Humphrey, 16 October 1855, in *Letters*, II, ed. Johnson, no. 180.

16. Letter cited by Anne Farnam "Woman Suffrage as an Alternative to the Beecher Ministry," in *Portraits of a Nineteenth Century Family*, ed. Earl A. French and Diana Royce (Hartford, Conn.: The Stowe-Day Foundation, 1976), p. 77.

17. Letter cited by Kathryn Kish Sklar, "Catharine Beecher's *A Treatise on Domestic Economy*," in *Portraits*, ed. French and Royce, p. 34.

18. From Jane Addams, *Twenty Years at Hull House*, 1910, in *The Oven Birds*, ed. Gail Parker, (New York: Doubleday, 1972), pp. 289–290.

19. Elizabeth Cady Stanton, *Eighty Years and More (1815–1897): Reminiscences of Elizabeth Cady Stanton* (New York: European Publishing Co., 1898), p. 20.

20. Ibid., p. 23.

21. Ibid., p. 147.

22. Ibid.

23. Ibid., p. 148.

24. Ibid.

25. Catharine E. Beecher, *Woman Suffrage and Woman's Profession* (Hartford, Conn.: Brown and Gross, 1871), p. 68.

26. Farnam, "Woman Suffrage," in *Portraits*, ed. French and Royce, p. 76.

27. Anne Throne Margolis, ed., *The Isabella Beecher Hooker Project* (Hartford, Conn.: The Stowe-Day Foundation, 1979), p. 14.

28. W. E. Brownlee and M. M. Brownlee, *Women in the American Economy* (New Haven, Conn.: Yale University Press, 1976), pp. 128–129.

29. Michele Clark, "Afterword," 8 December 1917, in Mary E. Wilkins Freeman, *The Revolt of Mother and Other Stories* (New York: The Feminist Press, 1974), p. 191.

30. Phyllis Chesler, *Women and Madness* (New York: Doubleday, 1972), pp. 18–19.

Chapter 4

1. M. H. Terhune, *Eve's Daughters* (New York: J. R. Anderson and H. S. Allen, 1882), p. 158.

2. M. B. Allen, M.D., and A. C. McGregor, M.D., *The Glory of Woman* (Philadelphia: Elliott Publishing Co., 1896), p. 86.

3. Edward H. Clarke, *Sex and Education: or A Fair Chance for the Girls* (Boston: Osgood, 1873), p. 39.

4. William Goodell, M.D., *The Dangers and the Duty of the Hour* (Philadelphia: S. M. Miller, Medical Publishers, 1882), p. 7.

5. Ibid., p. 5.

6. Ibid., p. 18.

7. Ibid., p. 8.

8. Ibid.

9. Allen and McGregor, *Glory*, p. 87.

10. Ibid., p. 89.

11. Bernard S. Talmey, M.D., *Woman* (New York, Stanley Press, 1906), p. 158.

12. MS to Mary Perkins, 11 October 1870, (Hartford, Conn.: The Stowe-Day Library).

13. Catharine E. Beecher, *Physiology and Calisthenics for Schools and Families* (New York: Harper and Brothers, 1856), p. 55.

14. Catharine E. Beecher and Harriet Beecher Stowe, *The American Woman's Home* (New York: J. B. Ford, 1869), pp. iv, 164.

15. Mrs. L. H. Sigourney, *Letters to Young Ladies* (Hartford, Conn.: William Watson, 1835), pp. 46–47.

Chapter 5

1. G. A. White, "The Private Letters of F. O. Matthiessen," *Harvard Magazine* (September–October 1978): 59.

2. "Communication from Mrs. R. B. Gleason," in Catharine Beecher, *Letters to the People on Health and Happiness*, 1855, reprinted in *Root of Bitterness*, ed. N. F. Cott, (New York: Dutton, 1972), p. 276.

3. Bernard S. Talmey, M.D., *Woman* (New York: Stanley Press, 1906), p. 158.

4. Ibid.

5. Talmey, *Woman*, p. 79.

6. Harvey Graham, *Eternal Eve, The History of Gynaecology and Obstetrics* (New York: Doubleday, 1951), pp. 435–436.

7. T. L. Nichols, M.D., and M. S. Gove Nichols, "Marriage, 1854," in *Root of Bitterness*, ed. N. F. Cott, p. 288.

8. Talmey, *Woman*, p. 158.

9. Graham, *Eternal Eve*, pp. 520–522.

Chapter 6

1. Carl N. Degler, *At Odds: Women and the Family in America from the Revolution to the Present* (New York: Oxford University Press, 1980), p. 22, from Diary of Lester Ward.

2. Peter Gay, *The Bourgeois Experience*, Vol. 1 (New York: Oxford University Press, 1984), p. 136.

3. Degler, *At Odds*, p. 267.

4. Ibid., p. 276.

5. Henry Putnam Stearns, *Insanity: Its Causes and Prevention* (New York: Putnam's, 1883), p. 190.

6. M. B. Allen, M.D., and A. C. McGregor, M.D., *The Glory of Woman* (Philadelphia: Elliott Publishing Co., 1896), p. 62.

7. Allen and McGregor, *Glory*, p. 104.

8. Ibid.

9. Ibid., p. 102.

10. Degler, *At Odds*, p. 268.

11. Ibid., p. 292.

12. Allen and McGregor, *Glory*, p. 103.

13. T. Stanton and H. S. Blatch, "Elizabeth Cady Stanton," in *The Oven Birds*, ed. Gail Parker (New York: Doubleday/Anchor, 1972), p. 267. Elizabeth Stanton made the entry in her diary in 1881.

14. Ibid., entry from 1883.

15. Rosalyn Baxandall, Linda Gordon, and Susan Reverby, *Amer-*

ica's Working Women (New York: Random House/Vintage, 1976), p. 93, from William Sanger, *A History of Prostitution* (New York: Harper Brothers, 1858).

16. Arlene Kisner, ed., *Woodhull and Claflin's Weekly: The Lives and Writings of Notorious Victoria Woodhull and Her Sister, Tennessee Claflin* (Washington, N.J.: Times Change Press, 1972), p. 30.; reprint of a letter dated November 23, 1871.

17. Lloyd Morris, *Incredible New York* (New York: Random House, 1951), p. 57. Cartoon is reproduced.

18. Baxandall, et al. *America's Working Women*, p. 93.

19. Gay, *Bourgeois Experience* p. 496.

20. Edith Wharton, *The Age of Innocence* (New York: D. Appleton, 1920), chapter 16.

21. Bernard L. Talmey, M.D., *Woman* (New York: Stanley Press, 1906), p. 9.

Chapter 7

1. C. K. Drinker, M.D., *Not So Long Ago, A Chronicle of Medicine and Doctors in Colonial Philadelphia* (New York: Oxford University Press, 1937), p. 4.

2. Harvey Graham, *Eternal Eve*, "The History of Gynecology and Obstetrics (New York: Doubleday, 1951), p. 446.

3. Ibid., p. 401.

4. Drinker, p. 85.

5. Ibid., p. 87.

6. Ibid., p. 59.

7. Quoted in Kathryn Kish Sklar, "Catharine Beecher's *A Treatise on Domestic Economy*," In Earl A. French and Diana Royce, eds., *Portraits of a Nineteenth Century Family* (Hartford: The Stowe-Day Foundation, 1976), p. 34.

8. William Goodell, M.D., *The Dangers and the Duty of the Hour* (Philadelphia: S. M. Miller, M.D., Medical Publishers, 1882), p. 22.

9. Goodell, p. 28.

10. Goodell, p. 17.

11. Victoria Woodhull, ed., *Woodhull and Claflin's Weekly*, November 2, 1872.

12. M. A. LaSorte, "Nineteenth Century Family Planning Practices," *The Journal of Psychohistory* 4 (Fall 1976): 165; Dr. E. B. Foote's *The Radical Remedy in Social Science* was published in 1886.

13. LaSorte, p. 171.

14. Rev. William Tatlock, "The Church's Duty in reference to the Criminal Classes," a sermon, Stamford, Conn., 1876. Connecticut

Historical Society, Hartford, Conn. Catharine Beecher also feared "the ignorant masses." *Woman's Suffrage and Woman's Profession* (Hartford, Conn.: Brown and Gross, 1871), p. 3.

15. W. Elliot Brownlee and Mary M. Brownlee, eds. *Women in the American Economy, A Documentary History, 1675 to 1929* (New Haven, Conn.: Yale University Press), p. 98.

16. Goodell, p. 26.

17. Bernard S. Talmey, M.D., *Woman* (New York: Stanley Press, 1906), p. 151.

18. LaSorte, p. 172.

19. Ibid., p. 170.

20. Carroll Smith-Rosenberg and Charles Rosenberg, "The Female Animal: Medical and Biological Views of Woman and Her Role in Nineteenth Century America," *The Journal of American History* 60 (September 1973): 350; from W. L. Atlee and D. A. O'Donnell, "Report of the Committee on Criminal Abortion," *Transactions of the American Medical Association*, 22 (1870): 241.

Chapter 8

1. M. B. Allen, M.D., and A. C. McGregor, M.D., *The Glory of Woman* (Philadelphia: Elliott Publishing, 1896), p. 53.

2. M. A. LaSorte, "Nineteenth Century Family Planning Practices," *Journal of Psychohistory* 4 (Fall 1976): 171.

3. Samuel Ashwell, *A Practical Treatise on the Diseases Peculiar to Women* (Boston: T. R. Marvin, 1843), p. 228.

4. Harriet Beecher Stowe, "The Lady Who Does Her Own Work," in *The Oven Birds*, ed. Gail Parker (New York: Doubleday/Anchor, 1972), p. 191.

5. MS, Harriet Beecher Stowe to Mary Perkins, 11 October 1870 (Hartford, Conn.: The Stowe-Day Library).

6. Harriet Beecher Stowe to Mrs. D. H. Allen, 2 December 1850, quoted by E. B. Kirkham, "Harriet Beecher Stowe, Autobiography and Legend," *Portraits of a Nineteenth Century Family*, ed. Earl A. French and Diana Royce (Hartford, Conn.: The Stowe-Day Foundation, 1976), p. 66.

7. Forrest Wilson, *Crusader in Crinoline, The Life of Harriet Beecher Stowe* (Philadelphia: J. B. Lippincott, 1941), p. 230.

8. Ibid., p. 338.

9. Lydia B. Sigourney, "Loss of Children," *Letters to Mothers* (Hartford, Conn.: Hudson and Skinner, 1838), pp. 210–211.

10. MS, Harriet Beecher Stowe to her husband, 3 February 1851 (Hartford, Conn.: The Stowe-Day Library).

11. Wilson, *Crusader*, p. 225.

12. Robert Etienne, "Ancient Medical Conscience and Children," *The Journal of Psychohistory* 4 (Fall 1976): 173.

13. Allen and McGregor, *Glory*, p. 276.

14. Bernard S. Talmey, M.D., *Woman* (New York: Stanley Press, 1906), p. 59.

15. Ann Throne Margolis, *The Isabella Beecher Hooker Project* (Hartford, Conn.: The Stowe-Day Foundation, 1979), p. 17.

16. Carroll Smith-Rosenberg, "The Hysterical Woman: Sex Roles and Role Conflict in 19th Century America," *Social Research* 39 (Winter 1972): 652.

17. Ibid., p. 662.

18. Allen and McGregor, *Glory*, p. 64.

19. Talmey, *Woman*, p. 81.

20. Charlotte Perkins Gilman, "The Yellow Wall-Paper," *New England Magazine* (January, 1892).

21. Henry James to Mrs. Henry James, Sr., 26 March 1870, *Letters*, Vol. I, ed. Leon Edel (Cambridge, Mass.: Belknap Press, 1974), pp. 218–219.

22. Alice James, *The Diary of Alice James*, ed. Leon Edel (New York: Dodd Mead, 1934, 1964), p. 81, 10 February 1890.

23. Ibid., p. 64, 11 December 1889.

24. Jean Strouse, *Alice James* (Boston: Houghton Mifflin, 1980), p. 304, letter of 6 July 1891.

25. Alice James, *Diary*, p. 36, 18 June 1889.

26. Ibid., p. 32, 12 June 1889.

27. Leon Edel, "Portrait of Alice James," in *Diary*, p. 8.

28. Alice James, *Diary*, p. 149, 26 October 1890.

29. Ibid., p. 149.

30. R. L. Moore, "The Spiritualist Medium: A Study of Female Professionalism in Victorian America," *American Quarterly*, 27 (May 1975): 207.

31. Ibid., p. 201.

32. Ibid., p. 205.

33. MS, Harriet Beecher Stowe to Mr. Garrison, 1868 (Hartford, Conn.: The Stowe-Day Library).

34. Moore, "Spiritualist Medium," p. 207.

35. *Woodhull and Claflin's Weekly*, New York, 2 November 1872.

36. Alice James, *Diary*, p. 231, 28 February 1892.

37. Moore, "Spiritualist Medium," p. 213.

38. Charlotte Perkins Gilman, "Women and Economics," in *The Feminist Papers*, ed. A. S. Rossi (New York: Columbia University Press/Bantam, 1974), p. 572.

39. E. F. Ellet, *The Queens of American Society* (Philadelphia: Porter and Coates, 1873) 6th ed., pp. 456–457.

40. Ibid., p. 452.

Chapter 9

1. Harvey Graham, *Eternal Eve: The History of Gynecology and Obstetrics* (New York: Doubleday, 1951), p. 508.

2. Ann Douglas, *The Feminization of American Culture* (New York: A. Knopf, 1977), pp. 332–339.

3. Elizabeth Cady Stanton, *Eighty Years and More (1815–1897) Reminiscences of Elizabeth Cady Stanton* (New York: European Publishing Company, 1898), pp. 146–147.

4. Carl N. Degler, *At Odds: Women and the Family in America from the Revolution to the Present* (New York: Oxford University Press), p. 318.

5. Ellsworth S. Grant, *The Colt Legacy* (Providence, R.I.: Mowbray Company, 1982), pp. 48–50.

Chapter 10

1. Statistics are from E. F. Baker, *Technology and Women's Work* (New York: Columbia University Press, 1964), pp. 75–77.

2. Rufus W. Griswold, ed., "Willimantic Railroad: Transplanted Bogs," *New England Weekly Gazette*, 24 February 1849.

3. Union for Home Work, Hartford, Conn., 1878, in Mabel C. Donnelly, *A Century of Service 1872–1972: Hartford Neighborhood Centers* (Hartford: Connecticut Printers, 1972), p. 14, Annual Report.

4. Rebecca Harding Davis, "Life in the Iron Mills," *Atlantic Monthly*, April 1861 in Tillie Olsen, *Silences* (New York: Delacorte/Seymour Lawrence, 1978), p. 267.

5. Jacob A. Riis, *How the Other Half Lives*, ed. S. B. Warner, Jr. (Cambridge, Mass.: Belknap Press, 1970), p. 83, 93.

6. *The American Woman's Home, with H. B. Stowe* (New York: J. B. Ford, 1869), p. 436.

7. Riis, *Other Half*, p. 4.

8. Ibid., p. 16.

9. Ibid., p. 44.

10. Ibid., p. 125.

11. Ibid., p. 117.

12. Ibid., p. 125.

13. Ibid., p. 127.

14. Ibid., p. 139.

15. Ibid., p. 142.

16. Ibid., p. 171.

17. Ibid., p. 6.

18. Ibid., p. 87.

19. R. Baxandall, L. Gordon, and S. Reverby, eds., *America's Working Women* (New York: Random House, 1976), p. 115.

20. Ibid., p. 157.

21. Elizabeth F. Baker, *Technology and Women's Work* (New York: Columbia University Press, 1964), p. 41.

22. Baxandall, et al., eds., *Working Women*, p. 108.

23. Letter by Terence Powderly of the Knights of Labor in *America's Working Women*, ed. R. Baxandall, L. Gordon, and S. Reverby (New York: Vintage/Random House, 1976), p. 125.

24. Philip S. Foner, ed., *Mother Jones Speaks, Collected Writings and Speeches* (New York: Monad Press, 1983), p. 5.

25. Baxandall, et al., eds., *Working Women*, p. 117.

26. Ibid., pp. 187–193; see Helen Marot, "A Woman's Strike—An Appreciation of the Shirtwaist Makers of New York."

27. W. E. Brownlee and M. M. Brownlee, eds. *Women in the American Economy* (New Haven, Conn.: Yale University Press, 1976), pp. 199–200.

28. Riis, *Other Half*, p. 154.

29. Brownlee and Brownlee, eds., *Women in the American Economy*, pp. 159–169.

30. Herman Melville, "The Tartarus of Maids," *Harper's New Monthly Magazine* X (April 1855): 675–676.

31. "Tuberculosis Harvest among Women in Cotton Mills," Summary of a study done by Dr. Perry on data from 1905–1907 from three New England mill towns, in the *New York Times*, June 29, 1913; reprinted in *Women: Their Changing Roles* (New York: New York Times/Arno Press, 1973), pp. 50–53.

32. Brownlee and Brownlee, eds., *Women in the American Economy*, p. 98.

33. Ibid., p. 129.

34. Victoria Woodhull, *Woodhull and Claflin's Weekly*, New York, November 2, 1872.

35. Baxandall, et al., eds. *America's Working Women*, from William W. Sanger, M.D., *A History of Prostitution* (New York: Harper Brothers, 1858), pp. 93–96.

36. Ellen Moers, *Literary Women* (New York: Doubleday/Anchor, 1977), p. 132.

37. Brownlee and Brownlee, eds., *Women in the American Economy*, p. 250.

38. Gerda Lerner, *Black Women in White America* (New York: Random House/Vintage, 1973), p. 99.

39. John Hope Franklin, "Harriet Tubman," in *Notable American Women*, Vol. 3 (Cambridge, Mass.: Belknap Press, 1971), p. 483.

40. Catharine Beecher, *Woman Suffrage and Woman's Profession* (Hartford, Conn.: Brown and Gross, 1871), p. 35.

41. Mabel C. Donnelly, *A Century of Service, 1872–1972: Hartford Neighborhood Centers* (Hartford: Connecticut Printers, 1972), p. 11.

42. MS, Harriet Beecher Stowe to Mary Perkins, 24 December 1855 (Hartford, Conn.: The Stowe-Day Library).

43. See Joseph S. Van Why, *Nook Farm* (Hartford, Conn.: The Stowe-Day Foundation, 1975).

44. Lerner, *Black Women*, p. 293.

45. L. H. Sigourney, *Whisper to a Bride* (Hartford, Conn.: Parsons, 1850), p. 35.

46. E. F. Ellet, *The New Cyclopedia of Domestic Economy* (Norwich, Conn.: Henry Bill Publishing, 1873), p. 45.

47. Riis, *Other Half*, p. 136.

48. Ibid., p. 191.

49. *300 Choice Receipts Compiled by the Ladies of Christ Church, Ansonia, Connecticut* (Hartford: Connecticut Historical Society, 1887).

50. E. B. Kirkham, "Harriet Beecher Stowe: Autobiography and Legend," in *Portraits of a Nineteenth Century Family*, ed. E. A. French and D. Royce (Hartford, Conn.: The Stowe-Day Foundation, 1976), p. 62.

51. Donnelly, *Century of Service*, p. 22.

52. Kirkham, "Harriet Beecher Stowe," p. 62.

53. Brownlee and Brownlee, ed., *Women in the American Economy*, pp. 99–100.

54. Ibid., p. 272.

55. Elizabeth Blackwell, "Pioneer Work in Opening the Medical Profession to Women," 1895, in *Women in the American Economy*, ed. Brownlee and Brownlee, pp. 273–275.

56. Brownlee and Brownlee, *Women in the American Economy*, pp. 288–296.

57. Belva Lockwood, "My Efforts to Become a Lawyer," in *Women in the American Economy*, ed. Brownlee and Brownlee, p. 298.

58. Louis Filler, "Belva Bennett McNall Lockwood," in *Notable American Women*, Vol. 2 (Cambridge, Mass.: Belknap Press, 1971), p. 414.

59. Catharine E. Beecher, *Woman Suffrage and Woman's Profession* (Hartford, Conn.: Brown and Gross, 1871), p. 11.

Chapter 11

1. Duncan Crow, *The Victorian Woman* (New York: Stein and Day, 1972), p. 175.
2. Elizabeth Cady Stanton, *Eighty Years and More (1815–1897): Reminiscences of Elizabeth Cady Stanton* (New York: European Publishing Company, 1898), p. 148.
3. Louis Filler, "Lucy Stone," in *Notable American Women*, Vol. III (Cambridge, Mass.: Belknap Press, 1971), p. 388.
4. Alice S. Rossi, ed., *The Feminist Papers: From Adams to de Beauvoir* (New York: Columbia University Press, 1973; reprint, New York: Bantam, 1974), pp. 291–292.
5. Alma Lutz, *Crusade for Freedom: Women in the Antislavery Movement* (Boston: Beacon Press, 1968), p. 44.
6. Stanton, *Eighty Years*, p. 162.
7. Ibid., p. 166.
8. Ibid., p. 257.
9. E. C. DuBois, *Feminism and Suffrage* (Ithaca, N.Y.: Cornell University Press, 1978), p. 104.
10. Ibid., p. 120.

Chapter 12

1. Raymond Lee Muncy, *Sex and Marriage in Utopian Communities, 19th-Century America* (Bloomington: Indiana University Press, 1973), p. 3.
2. Jonathan Beecher and Richard Bienvenu, eds. and trans., *The Utopian Vision of Charles Fourier* (Boston: Beacon Press, 1972), p. 20.
3. Beecher and Bienvenu, *Utopian Vision* p. 216.
4. Muncy, *Sex and Marriage*, p. 175.
5. Ibid., p. 22.
6. Ibid., p. 218.

Chapter 13

1. Catharine Beecher, *Woman Suffrage and Woman's Profession* (Hartford, Conn.: Brown and Gross, 1871), p. 18.
2. Ibid., p. 3.

3. Hartford, Connecticut *Courant*, October 29, 1869.

4. Elizabeth Cady Stanton to Susan B. Anthony, 10 September 1855, in *The Oven Birds*, ed. Gail Parker (New York: Doubleday/Anchor, 1972), p. 262.

5. Ibid., pp. 264–265.

6. *The Complete Essays of Montaigne*, Vol. I, trans. Donald M. Frame (Stanford, Calif.: Stanford University Press, 1958), p. 138.

7. Hertha Pauli, *Her Name Was Sojourner Truth* (New York: Appleton-Century-Crofts, 1962), p. 189.

8. Alice S. Rossi, ed., *The Feminist Papers* (New York: Columbia University Press/Bantam, 1974), p. 151.

9. Ibid., p. 169.

10. Ibid., p. 182.

11. Elizabeth Cady Stanton to Susan B. Anthony, 2 April 1852, "My Dear Friend," in *The Oven Birds*, ed. Gail Parker (New York: Doubleday/Anchor, 1972), p. 260.

12. Rossi, ed., *Feminist Papers*, p. 382.

13. Ibid.

14. Ibid., p. 381.

Chapter 14

1. Elizabeth Cady Stanton, Susan B. Anthony, and Matilda Joslyn Gage, "Preface," *History of Woman Suffrage*, II (New York: Fowler and Wells, 1881), p. vi.

2. L. S. Sigourney, *Whisper to a Bride* (Hartford: H. S. Parsons Co., 1850), p. 5.

3. Elizabeth Cady Stanton, *Eighty Years and More (1815–1897), Reminiscences of Elizabeth Cady Stanton* (New York: European Publishing Company, 1898), p. 165.

4. Catharine E. Beecher and Harriet Beecher Stowe, *The American Woman's Home* (New York: J. B. Ford, 1869), p. i. See also p. 19.

5. Stanton, *Eighty Years and More*, p. 255.

6. Carl N. Degler, *At Odds: Women and the Family in America from the Revolution to the Present* (New York: Oxford University Press, 1980), p. 318.

7. Alice S. Rossi, ed., *The Feminist Papers* (New York: Columbia University Press/Bantam, 1974), p. 592; See also Charlotte Perkins Gilman, *Women and Economics* (Boston: Small, Maynard, 1898).

8. Rossi, ed., *Feminist Papers*, p. 591.

9. Ibid., p. 587.

BIBLIOGRAPHY

Addams, Jane. *Twenty Years at Hull House*. New York: Macmillan, 1910.

Allen, Monfort B., M.D. and Amelia C. McGregor, M.D. *The Glory of Woman*. Philadelphia: Elliott Publishing Co., 1896.

Ashwell, Samuel, M.D. *A Practical Treatise on the Diseases Peculiar to Women*. Boston: T. R. Marvin, 1843.

Baker, Elizabeth Faulkner. *Technology and Woman's Work*. New York: Columbia University Press, 1964.

Baker, William J., ed. *America Perceived: A View from Abroad in the 19th Century*. West Haven, Conn.: Pendulum Press, 1974.

Baxandall, Rosalyn, Linda Gordon, and Susan Reverby, eds. *America's Working Women*. New York: Vintage/Random House, 1976.

Baym, Nina. *Woman's Fiction, A Guide to Novels by and about Women in America, 1820–1870*. Ithaca, N.Y.: Cornell University Press, 1978.

Beecher, Catharine E. *Physiology and Calisthenics for Schools and Families*. New York: Harper and Brothers, 1856.

———. *Woman Suffrage and Woman's Profession*. Hartford, Conn.: Brown and Gross, 1871.

Beecher, Catharine E., and Harriet Beecher Stowe. *The American Woman's Home*. New York: J. B. Ford, 1869.

Beecher, Jonathan, and Richard Bienvenu, eds. and trans. *The Utopian Vision of Charles Fourier*. Boston: Beacon Press, 1971.

Berg, Barbara J. *The Remembered Gate: Origins of American Feminism, The Woman and the City, 1800–1860*. New York: Oxford University Press, 1978.

Brownlee, W. Elliot, and Mary M. Brownlee, eds. *Women in the*

American Economy, A Documentary History, 1675–1929. New Haven, Conn.: Yale University Press, 1976.

Buhle, MariJo, and Paul Buhle. *The Concise History of Woman Suffrage, Selections from the Classic Work of Stanton, Anthony, Gage, and Harper*. Urbana: University of Illinois Press, 1978.

Chesler, Phyllis. *Women and Madness*. New York: Doubleday, 1972.

Clark, Michele. "Afterword." In *The Revolt of Mother and Other Stories*, ed. Mary E. Wilkins Freeman. New York: The Feminist Press, 1974.

Clarke, Edward H. *Sex and Education; or a Fair Chance for the Girls*. Boston: Osgood, 1873.

Cott, Nancy F., ed. *Root of Bitterness: Documents of the Social History of American Women*. New York: Dutton, 1972.

Crow, Duncan. *The Victorian Woman*. New York: Stein and Day, 1972.

Dalessio, D. J., M.D. "Hyperventilation, The Vapors, Effort Syndrome, Neurasthenia." *Journal of the American Medical Association* 239 (April 1978): 1401–1402.

Degler, Carl N. *At Odds: Women and the Family in America from the Revolution to the Present*. New York: Oxford University Press, 1980.

Dodden, Faye E. *Serving Women: Household Service in Nineteenth Century America*. Middletown, Conn.: Wesleyan University Press, 1983.

Donnelly, Mabel C. *A Century of Service, 1872–1972: Hartford Neighborhood Centers*. Hartford: Connecticut Printers, 1972.

Douglas, Ann. *The Feminization of American Culture*. New York: A. Knopf, 1977.

Drinker, C. K., M.D. *Not So Long Ago: A Chronicle of Medicine and Doctors in Colonial Philadelphia*. New York: Oxford University Press, 1937.

DuBois, Ellen Carol. *Feminism and Suffrage: The Emergence of the Independent Women's Movement in America*. Ithaca, N.Y.: Cornell University Press, 1978.

Edel, Leon, ed. *The Diary of Alice James*. New York: Dodd Mead, 1934.

——. *Henry James Letters*, Vol. I, Cambridge, Mass.: Belknap Press, 1974.

Ellet, Mrs. E. F.[Elizabeth Lummis]. *The New Cyclopedia of Domestic Economy*. Norwich, Conn.: Henry Bill Publishing, 1873.

——. *The Queens of American Society*, 6th ed. Philadelphia: Porter and Coates, 1873.

Etienne, Robert. "Ancient Medical Conscience and Children" *The Journal of Psychohistory* 4 (1976): 131–157.

Farnam, Anne. "Woman Suffrage as an Alternative to the Beecher

Ministry." In *Portraits of a Nineteenth Century Family*, ed. Earl A. French and Diana Royce. Hartford, Conn.: The Stowe-Day Foundation, 1976.

Finley, Martha. *Elsie's Girlhood*. New York: Dodd, Mead, 1872.

Foner, Philip S., ed. *Mother Jones Speaks*. New York: Monad Press, 1983.

Frame, Donald M., trans. *The Complete Essays of Montaigne*. Stanford, Calif.: Stanford University Press, 1958.

Franklin, John Hope. "Harriet Tubman" *Notable American Women*, Vol. 3. Cambridge, Mass.: The Belknap Press of Harvard University Press, 1971.

Garland, Hamlin. *Main-Travelled Roads*. 1891. New York: Signet/New American Library, 1962.

Gay, Peter. *The Bourgeois Experience*, Vol. 1. New York: Oxford University Press, 1984.

Geller, Jeffrey L., M.D. "Women's Accounts of Psychiatric Illness and Institutionalization." *Hospitals and Community Psychiatry* 36 (October 1985): 1056–1062.

Gilman, Charlotte Perkins. "Women and Economics." In *The Feminist Papers*, ed. Alice A. Rossi. New York: Columbia University Press, 1973, New York: Bantam, 1974.

Gold, Michael. *Jews without Money*. New York: Horace Liveright, 1930; and New York: Avon Books, 1965.

Goodell, William, M.D. *The Dangers and the Duty of the Hour*. Philadelphia: S. M. Miller, M.D., Medical Publishers, 1882.

Graham, Harvey. *Eternal Eve: The History of Gynaecology and Obstetrics*. New York: Doubleday, 1951.

Grant, Ellsworth S. *The Colt Legacy*. Providence, R.I.: Mowbray Company, 1982.

Hale, S. J., ed. *The Juvenile Miscellany*. Boston: E. R. Broaders, 1835.

Hartford Daily Courant, May 7–15, 1869, May 10, 15, 1889.

Hartford Daily Times, May 12, 1869.

[Hoffmann, Heinrich.] *Struwwelpeter, Merry Stories and Funny Pictures*. London: Blackie, n.d.

James, Howard T., ed. *Notable American Women, 1607–1950*, 3 vols. Cambridge, Mass.: Belknap Press, 1971.

Jeffrey, Julie Roy. *Frontier Women, the Trans-Mississippi West, 1840–1880*. New York: Hill and Wang, 1979.

Johnson, Thomas H., ed. *The Letters of Emily Dickinson*. 3 vols. Cambridge, Mass.: Belknap Press, 1958.

Kirkham, E. Bruce. "Harriet Beecher Stowe." In *Portraits of a Nineteenth Century Family*, ed. Earl A. French and Diana Royce. Hartford, Conn.: The Stowe-Day Foundation, 1976.

Kisner, Arlene, ed. *Woodhull and Claflin's Weekly: The Lives and*

Writings of Notorious Victoria Woodhull and Her Sister Tennessee Claflin. Washington, N.J.: Times Change Press, 1972.

LaSorte, M. A. "Nineteenth Century Family Planning Practices." *Journal of Psychohistory* 4 (1976): 163–183.

Lerner, Gerda, ed., *Black Women in White America, A Documentary History.* New York: Vintage Books/Random House, 1972.

Lutz, Alma. *Crusade for Freedom: Women of the Anti-Slavery Movement.* Boston: Beacon, 1968.

Margolis, Anne Throne. *The Isabella Beecher Hooker Project.* Hartford, Conn.: The Stowe-Day Foundation, 1979.

Melville, Herman. "The Tartarus of Maids." *Harpers New Monthly Magazine* (April 1855): 673–678.

Millett, Kate. *Sexual Politics.* New York: Doubleday, 1970.

Moers, Ellen. *Literary Women.* New York: Anchor/Doubleday, 1977.

Moore, R. L. "The Spiritualist Medium: A Study of Female Professionalism in Victorian America." *American Quarterly* 27 (1975): 200–221.

Morris, Lloyd. *Incredible New York.* New York: Random House, 1951.

Muncy, Raymond Lee. *Sex and Marriage in Utopian Communities, 19th Century America.* Bloomington: Indiana University Press, 1973.

Myres, Sandra L. *Westering Women and the Frontier Experience.* Albuquerque: University of New Mexico Press, 1982.

Olsen, Tillie. *Silences.* New York: Delacorte/Seymour Lawrence, 1978.

Ossoli, Margaret Fuller. *Woman in the Nineteenth Century.* Westport, Conn.: Greenwood Press, 1968; reprinted from Roberts Press edition, 1874.

Parker, Gail., ed. *The Oven Birds, American Women on Womanhood, 1820–1920.* New York: Anchor/Doubleday, 1972.

Pauli, Hertha. *Her Name Was Sojourner Truth.* New York: Appleton-Century-Crofts, 1962.

Pierpont, John. *Exercises in Reading and Recitation.* Boston: Charles Bowen, 1836.

Riis, Jacob A. *How the Other Half Lives.* ed. S. B. Warner, Jr. Cambridge, Mass.: Belknap Press, 1970.

———. *How the Other Half Lives.* New York: Dover, 1971. Book of one hundred photographs from the Jacob A. Riis Collection, The Museum of the City of New York. Page references are to the Belknap Press edition.

Rossi, Alice A., ed. *The Feminist Papers: From Addams to de Beauvoir.* New York: Columbia University Press, 1973; New York: Bantam, 1974. Pagination is identical in both editions.

Schneir, Miriam, ed. *Feminism, The Essential Historical Writings.* New York: Random House, 1972.

Sears, Hal D. *The Sex Radicals, Free Love in High Victorian America*. Lawrence: The Regents Press of Kansas, 1977.

Sigourney, L. H. *Letters to Young Ladies*. Hartford, Conn.: William Watson, 1835.

———. "Loss of Children." In *Letters to Mothers*. Hartford, Conn.: Hudson and Skinner, 1838.

———. *Whisper to a Bride*. Hartford, Conn.: H. S. Parsons, 1850.

Sklar, Kathryn Kish. "Catharine Beecher's A Treatise on Domestic Economy." In *Portraits of a Nineteenth Century Family*, ed. Earl A. French and Diana Royce. Hartford, Conn.: The Stowe-Day Foundation, 1976.

Smith, Page. *Daughters of the Promised Land*. Boston: Little Brown, 1970.

Smith-Rosenberg, Carroll. "The Female World of Love and Ritual: Relations between Women in Nineteenth-Century America." *Signs: Journal of Women in Culture and Society* 1 (1975): 1–29.

———. "The Hysterical Woman: Sex Roles and Role Conflict in Nineteenth-Century America." *Social Research* 10 (1972): 652–678.

Smith-Rosenberg, Carroll, and Charles Rosenberg. "The Female Animal: Medical and Biological Views of Woman and Her Role in Nineteenth-Century America." *Journal of American History* 60 (1973): 332–356.

Stanton, Elizabeth Cady. *Eighty Years and More (1815–1897): Reminiscences of Elizabeth Cady Stanton*. New York: European Publishing Company, 1898.

Stanton, Elizabeth Cady, Susan B. Anthony and Matilda Joslyn Gage. *History of Woman Suffrage*, Vol. 2. New York: Fowler and Wells, 1881.

Stearns, H. P., M.D. *Insanity: Its Causes and Prevention*. New York: Putnam's, 1883.

Stern, Madeline, B., ed. *The Victoria Woodhull Reader*. Weston, Mass.: M & S Press, 1974.

Stowe, Harriet Beecher. MS letters: 3 February 1851 to Calvin Stowe; 24 December 1855 to Mary Beecher Perkins; 17 July 1864 to Lydia Beecher; 1868 to Lloyd Garrison; 11 October 1870 to Mary Beecher Perkins. Hartford, Conn.: The Stowe-Day Library.

Strouse, Jean. *Alice James*. Boston: Houghton Mifflin, 1980.

Sumner, Helen L. *History of Women in Industry in the United States*. New York: Arno Press, 1974; from 1910 Bureau of Labor Statistics.

Talmey, Bernard, S., M.D. *Woman*. New York: Stanley Press, 1906.

Tatlock, Rev. William. "The Church's Duty in reference to the Criminal Classes." Sermon given in Stamford, Conn., 1876. Hartford, Conn.: Connecticut Historical Society.

Terhune, Marion Harland. *Eve's Daughters, or Common Sense for Maid, Wife, and Mother*. New York: J. R. Anderson and H. S. Allen, 1882.

300 Choice Receipts, compiled by The Ladies of Christ Church. Ansonia, Conn.: 1887. In the Connecticut Historical Society, Hartford, Conn.

"Tuberculosis Harvest Among Women in Cotton Mills. "Summary of a study done by Dr. Perry on data from 1905–1907 from three New England mill towns." *New York Times* June 29, 1913. Reprinted in *Women: Their Changing Roles*, ed. Elizabeth Janeway. New York: New York Times/Arno Press, 1973.

Van Why, Joseph S. *Nook Farm*. Hartford, Conn.: The Stowe-Day Foundation, 1975.

The Well Bred Boy. Boston: William Crosby and Co., 1839.

White, G. A. "The Private Letters of an American Scholar, F. O. Matthiessen," *Harvard Magazine* 81 (September-October 1978): 58–62.

"Willimantic Railroad: Transplanted Bogs." *The New England Weekly Gazette*, February 24, 1849. Hartford, Conn.

Wilson, Forrest. *Crusader in Crinoline, The Life of Harriet Beecher Stowe*. Philadelphia: J. B. Lippincott Co., 1941.

Wood, Ann Douglas. "The Fashionable Diseases." *Journal of Interdisciplinary History* 4 (1973): 25–52.

Woodhull and Claflin's Weekly. 5 (November 2, 1872): 10–13. Excerpts from other issues found in Arlene Kisner, ed. *Woodhull and Claflin's Weekly*, 1972; and in Madeline Stern, ed. *The Victoria Woodhull Reader*, 1974.

Wright, Richard. *Black Boy*. New York: Harper and Row, 1937.

INDEX